Head to HoD

Improving the management of Departments

edited by
Vivian Anthony and John M Moore

John Catt Educational Limited

Managing Director: Jonathan Evans – Editor in Chief: Derek Bingham

Head to HoD
First Published 1998

by John Catt Educational Ltd.
Great Glemham, Saxmundham, Suffolk IP17 2DH
Tel: 01728 663666 Fax: 01728 663415 E-mail: enq@johncatt.co.uk

©1998 John Catt Educational Ltd.

ISBN: 0 901577 21 9

Designed and typeset by
John Catt Educational Limited

Printed and bound in Great Britain by Bell and Bain Ltd, Glasgow, Scotland.

Contents

Foreword

Chris Woodhead
HM Chief Inspector of Schools

We live in interesting and rapidly changing educational times. Nothing is sacred. One controversy follows hard on the heels of its predecessor. I could well understand if those of you who work in HMC schools were to conclude that the best strategy is to lock your classroom doors and wait for the wheel to come full circle.

I hope, though, that you do not do this. The debate will be richer for your contribution. There is a chance that the conclusions will be more sensible. There is the fact, too, that if HMC does not involve itself, then it has only itself to blame if policies emerge which impact adversely on the quality of education you can provide in your schools.

I welcome, therefore, this book. It covers the ground in a systematic way and touches on most of the key issues of the moment. It ought to inspire and it may well provoke. It will certainly alert all who read it to developments which, for better or worse, will have a profound effect on both state and independent schools.

There are, for example, some key decisions to be made on the shape of the post-16 curriculum. I personally very much hope that we do not see a lowering of expectation. We must, of course, provide more intelligible, more demanding and more relevant courses for those students who are unlikely to benefit from traditional A level study. But let us recognise that the intense and rigorous study of a small number of subjects is absolutely right for some of our most academically gifted students. To deny these students the opportunity to develop their gifts would be a tragic and retrograde step.

We need to hold hard to two obvious truths. The first is that education is, or ought to be, as Oakeshott put it, a conversation between the generations in which the young are initiated into those aspects of our culture which are worth preserving. The second is that everything depends upon the humanity and expectation and professional good sense of the individual teacher It is the teacher in his or her classroom that matters, not the Secretary of State or the Chief Inspector of Schools.

There are many who want to undermine education as Oakeshott conceived it. That is why I hope this book is read widely. The better informed the individual teacher, the stronger and hopefully wiser the collective professional voice.

Preface

Dr Nicholas Tate
Chief Executive, Qualifications & Curriculum Authority

It is a truism to suggest that the quality of a school depends crucially on the quality of its managers. We hear a great deal these days about the quality of management and its role in promoting school effectiveness and improvement, but it is mostly Heads we hear about. Although their role in providing a vision and effective leadership is of course vital, so too is that of other managers in the school, and above all Heads of Departments.

A good Head delegates maximum responsibility to Heads of Departments within a framework of common policies and accountability. To exercise these responsibilities, Heads of Departments also need vision: both a vision of what their subject uniquely can contribute to the overall education of pupils and a sense of how it fits within the wider curriculum and in relation to the school's broader objectives. I very much welcome therefore a publication which encourages Heads of Departments to think about their role. I always feel that the curriculum is a statement of what one generation values sufficiently to wish to pass it on to the next. If this is so, we cannot separate it from our wider vision of the kind of society we are preparing young people to join and from the values and assumptions we are trying to transmit. If this book encourages Heads of Departments to think about these things, alongside more practical matters, it will have been well worthwhile.

Introduction

Vivian Anthony

One theme emerging from this book and the large number of inspection reports on HMC schools is the central role of middle management in bringing about school improvement. If the importance of Heads of Departments has been undervalued in the past they are now placed firmly at the heart of lines of communication in the school. The policies worked out by Governors and the Senior Management Team have to be implemented at the departmental level. The Head of Department has to lead his team in finding the most effective ways of carrying out the plans.

While all those who contributed to this volume have attended meetings of the HMC Academic Policy Sub-Committee at one time or another, there has been no attempt to instruct the writers to follow structures or guidelines. They were asked to think of Heads of Department when they were writing. This led to some chapters about curricular developments, while others were about courses and assessment. Educational technologies and strategic devices for school improvement feature alongside information about the agencies established to promote 'a world class education service'. We have been constantly reminded that success depends on the quality of those in the front line – Heads of Department and the other classroom teachers.

What a role we expect of them! At their regular departmental meeting – minuted now, of course – they must endeavour to keep their colleagues up to scratch on all the latest developments and threatened changes. How should they respond to the proposal that there should be less teaching time for their subject so that more time can be spent on Key Skills or on otherwise broadening the curriculum? What ideas does the department have for applying ICT in teaching their subjects? Other departments have adopted modular schemes and this is having an effect on their subject.

A trainee teacher will be joining the department next term and will need a mentor and opportunities to develop essential competences. The junior member of the department has to be appraised and subsequently suitable professional development courses have to be found for her. Departmental schemes of work need to be updated in preparation for next year's inspection and cover has to be found for the Number Two who will be away for a week on inspection. The budget is already nearly spent and there is a term to go in which the department has to find resources for its part in the Sixth Form general studies programme. The Headmaster has received the results of the appeal against last year's GCSE results and he is still not happy, nor are the parents. Your contribution to your subject association's journal entitled 'How to become an HoD and have an easy life' is due next week. Promotion must be the answer.

When John Moore and I discussed the contributions in this book – and we are most grateful to the authors for finding time in busy schedules – he thought more should be said of the centrality of the role of the Head of Department. Of course, they must know their subject well and how to deliver it, but they must also have ability to lead – to do whatever is necessary to get the best out of the other members of the department, while sharing fairly the plums and the suffering. The knack of deploying them where they will teach best, while using new challenges as an effective form of staff development, is the key to success.

He thought that meetings were also a key part of the role of a Head of Department and commented "Departmental meetings should be at the centre of a successful department, but at least as important are Heads of Department meetings, academic committees and so on. Of course, Heads of Department must defend their departmental corner in such meetings. Any Head would expect that, and expect the arguments deployed to be as logical as they were forceful, but he or she would also hope that any Head of Department will have (or develop!) a wider vision. Some elements of such meetings are inevitably routine – nuts and bolts – but the important discussions are those crossing subject boundaries or with a bearing on the curriculum as a whole. It is here that a good Head of Department will appreciate the needs of other departments and be able to look beyond the narrow interests of his own subject to the wider picture. Such people are of inestimable value to Heads and Directors of Studies trying to generate a vision for the academic side of a school or aiming to develop a consensus about the handling of curriculum change – and there will be a fair bit of that over the next few years! The key to success is the constructive meeting of minds. It is also useful to remember that it does not take much brain or ingenuity to ask the unanswerable and/or destructive question; the perceptive and constructive suggestion in discussion is gold dust ..."

Heads of Department are not on their own. Support structures are either in place or are being established. Inspectors are at pains to ascertain how well they work. Internally the Head and the Director of Studies must maintain good lines of communication. Occasionally these can become obscured by the activities of powerful Heads of Year or Heads of House. Departments must know how they fit into the greater scheme of things. Their contributions to school development plans for the medium term, and action plans in the short term, are essential. They must set targets for improvement which accord with these plans and are realistic.

A process of monitoring and assessment is fundamental to every effective department. The Head of Department must know how well his colleagues are teaching and performing other professional duties like preparation and marking. Is the department's marking policy in line with that for the rest of the school and is it being adhered to? There must be an overview of the progress being made by all pupils in the department. Are they obtaining results in line with expectations, even if some of them have only modest ability in the subject? Other pupils with outstanding ability may not have enough to keep them stimulated. It must address the problem of boys' performance falling behind that of girls. The department must be alive to new methods of teaching the subject and new courses which become available. Should the relevant GNVQ course be introduced?

HMC exists first and foremost to help to meet the needs of Headmasters and Headmistresses. However, those needs include providing for the professional development of their staff. The Academic Policy Sub–Committee has been addressing the main issues and producing briefing papers for the past decade. Throughout that period there have been detailed discussions of the reform of post-16 education. Indeed, such discussions have been going on throughout my career in education which began in 1960! The aim has been to keep Heads and Heads of Department informed of proposals for change and to make sure that those with the power to bring about these changes are aware of the views of teachers in our schools. For HMC schools, which send 95% of the pupils on to universities, it is essential to influence Vice-Chancellors and admissions tutors. They share with HMC the desire to maintain rigour and intellectual challenge in Sixth Form courses but without their support it will be difficult to achieve any broadening of students' programmes. The HMC/GSA University Working Party represents members' interests and provides a flow of information in both directions.

This book is part of the process of disseminating information. It points to help that is forthcoming from other agencies and draws on the findings of leading exponents in different fields of education. Keeping abreast of the publications of QCA and the Examination Boards, of OFSTED and the inspection services for independent schools, of the TTA and training practitioners, of the CEM Centre at Durham University and other schemes like the National Grid for Learning is no small challenge. The DfEE will continue with its policy of 'death by a hundred consultations' but they cannot be ignored. The purpose of this book is to pass on some of the wisdom and experience of twelve Heads who continue to struggle with the same issues which face Heads of Department on a regular basis. We hope it helps.

Chapter 1

The Curriculum: reflection, reaction and crystal gazing

John M Moore

Headmaster, The King's School, Worcester

This is no place for too much reminiscing, but one way of leading into some thoughts about what might be sensible aspirations for education in the broadest sense and, within that, for the curriculum of the future, is to start with a look back at how things have developed in my time. If nothing else, it may show where I come from and that surely has some bearing on the ideas which I shall put forward.

The Stone Age

After initial wartime disruption because of which I attended ten schools before the age of 12 – a process which seemed to do far less damage than any of today's parents would ever believe – I ended up at Rugby too young, but allegedly able to cope. There I was immediately offered the one option available on the timetable at that point: a choice between Greek, German and Science. The starkness of this choice was somehow underlined when it transpired that Geography was only taught in one set of forms in the whole school, which in my case meant for just one term in my whole career. The curious nature of these arrangements was compounded by the fact that pupils were promoted termly if their progress justified it. How any coherence was maintained I cannot think.

The introduction of O levels by the post-war Labour Government also had its impact. When that examination replaced the School Certificate, no-one was allowed to take it until they were aged 16. This restriction was designed by the Government of the day to ensure that all those at Secondary Modern Schools would have left school (at the school leaving age of 15) before they could sit O levels; thus there could be no odious comparisons between their performance and that of Grammar School pupils. Because of the age limit, Rugby decided to put almost all members of the School who had not taken it already through the last School Certificate in November 1949. We were not told we were taking it until the end of

John M Moore was educated at Rugby and Clare College, Cambridge obtaining MA and PhD degrees in Classics. His teaching career was at Winchester College (1960-64) and Radley College (1964-83) where he was Head of Classics and Director of Sixth Form. He became Headmaster of The King's School, Worcester in 1983. He served on the Academic Policy Sub-Committee from 1987 and was Chairman (1995-98). His interests include watercolours, painting, travel and being a JP.

October, which ensured that we took the papers without any of the tension and apprehension which is generated these days by the battery of dire warnings and mock papers which the modern world seems to think are essential to success. This was good, but it also meant that I ended up in the Sixth Form at the age of 14. This might not have happened had it not been for the advent of O level, but it was no more than an extension of the school's policy of promoting pupils by achievement and on a judgement of whether they were ready for the next stage, not according to their calendar age.

At that time, the school, like almost every other, was divided at O level into three 'sides': Classics, Modern and Science. On each side, there were four forms; A levels (also just introduced) were taken by those who needed to take them at the third level, and the fourth was broadly reserved for those expected to get awards to Oxbridge. Having opted for Greek, I naturally joined the Classics side, and had a thoroughly enjoyable time. In our specialist subjects we were superbly trained and often taught well too – and by the end were very fluent in Latin and Greek, and also knew some Ancient History. We were in fact so well trained that the first year at university was not remotely demanding, and therefore gave opportunities to go to lectures in other subjects and to read widely; but what about broader education within the schooling I received?

Examinations, even those required for Oxford and Cambridge Scholarships and entrance, did not loom anything like so large on our horizons as they do now, and there were admirable ways of broadening what one studied. In addition to specialist work, everyone did English and Religious Studies throughout their time at school, and these subjects were well taught and included more than an element of philosophy. We were also required to learn a minimum of 30 lines of verse a week – Latin, Greek or English; still useful for *The Times* Crossword, but I am sure of much wider educational value than that. Further, there were periods set aside each week for 'additional' subjects in which a raft of options was on offer; for me A level Mathematics and a couple of in-depth science courses, for others Languages, Art or a wide range of what are now sometimes called 'complementary studies'. Apart from that, because our specialist work was spread over a longer period and was not so examination-driven, there was considerable breadth as well as depth in what we studied. I doubt if many would defend such a system and curriculum today, but it was neither as rigid nor as narrow as it appeared on the surface. Inherent in that is an important point: it is wrong to judge the breadth or the depth of any particular subject or combination of subjects without looking not merely at what subjects and how many are included, but within them at what they contain and how they are presented – at the totality of the learning experience. Good teachers educate, they do not just cover the syllabus, and to do that they need 'space'.

The Bronze Age

Six years after leaving school I started teaching, and a not dissimilar system applied, though by then very few pupils specialised as early as I had, even in the flexible system at Winchester College. Pupils still moved up according to achievement, not age, with termly promotions at least possible and often occurring. There was a clear focus on university ambitions rather than A levels which were often taken *en passant* at least a year before the serious stuff of Oxford or Cambridge entrance. Breadth came much as at Rugby, and we had rare and infinitely exciting flexibility such as people in the same form doing Latin, Greek and Double Mathematics and deciding at the last moment which to offer for an Oxbridge scholarship. There were also scientists who won the very demanding College English literature prizes. But that was Winchester.

On moving to what were then perhaps less rarified pastures at Radley, I found much was the same, though without termly promotions, which made it easier as a Head of Department to design some coherence in our courses. This, however, was the time when the old division of subjects into three groups was being questioned, and the first 'blocking systems' were coming in. This change was at least important enough to justify describing it as a major step forward. Of course not every combination could or should be made possible in any blocking system, despite the passionate arguments I once faced from a pupil who had some crazy logic behind his desire to combine A levels in Greek, Chemistry and Art. No longer did every pupil on the 'modern' side have to do History; most of my Classical Sixth were freed to take Mathematics, English or a Modern Language with their Latin and Greek and, while some of them did Ancient History, the majority of the (large) Ancient History sets were drawn from those doing English, Modern Languages and so on – and even the occasional scientist joined us.

Life up to O level was much the same as it had been, though everyone did an early form of dual-award science, and Greek and German were two options among many. Thus, the earlier years were a lot more sensible than the curriculum I had suffered – no, actually enjoyed! – and this was followed by a significant degree of flexibility in the Sixth Form curriculum; not before time! There was also an inherent freedom in all teaching, particularly in the Sixth Form, because parents and pupils were not obsessed with the syllabus. The pernicious practice of parents buying examination syllabuses, passing them to their offspring and then questioning the 'relevance' of everything taught which they could not see listed in what was published by the Examination Boards was, at least for me, unknown. There was more hunger for ideas, an interest in knowledge for its own sake, and a willingness to digress on everyone's part which may have caused the odd disaster when misused, but which also certainly led to some really stimulating and broad education.

There was a General Studies course in the Sixth Form; it was 'home-grown' and its format and content differed from year to year; it was not examined, but it did broaden everyone's horizons. As well as that, three periods a week of Additional Subjects were timetabled at the same time across the whole Sixth Form in which up to 40 courses were offered ranging from O level resits to Modern Languages, Astronomy, Byzantine Art, Cooking and Car Maintenance; there was breadth there for those who were prepared to look for it. A further broadening element for the ablest pupils in those days was the extra term, or occasionally four terms, which led to Oxford or Cambridge Entrance. The post-A level Third Year Sixth had a freedom which even then was not possible within the A level courses, and many pupils and teachers found this the most stimulating part of what they did.

Another important change came about during those years: accelerated promotion for the abler became rarer and rarer, moving over ten years from 60% of the entry taking O levels after two years rather than three to 20%, and shortly after I left to none. This change posed challenges in the classroom which are still with us in terms of keeping interested and excited the over-trained and sometimes precocious products of preparatory schools, notably those with good and large scholarship streams, but it did and does give scope to broaden within the syllabus of each subject.

The Iron Age

As time passed, there was increasing dissatisfaction with A levels – for precisely the reasons which lay behind the most recent proposals for reform. Replacements were mooted – Q and F, N and F and I level – and some of us spent a lot of time on these various proposals, all of which were designed to broaden the post-16 curriculum, and all of which were torpedoed by one interest group or another at university level which was convinced it could not risk any drop in the supposed standards achieved by their potential entrants. We almost got change when the Higginson Report recommended that all should do five leaner but demanding 'new' A levels, but that recommendation fell foul of a famous handbag. While I was excited by it at the time, as were many, I am not now sure that it was the right answer even then, and it certainly would not solve our problems in a very different world today.

Meanwhile, a very different issue became pressing. Just as A levels had been designed for the top 6-10% of the ability range, so O levels had been intended for the 'academic' only. What is more, O level had been designed to act as an external guarantee of a reasonably broad pre-A level education, and the original plan was that subjects to be taken at A level would be bypassed, not even taken, at O level. That idea was virtually still-born because of the uncertainty of the great majority of the candidates about their A level choices even at the time when examination entries had to be made – but it had its point even if only in theory.

In parallel with O levels, the rest of the world was offered the CSE. Many CSEs were excellent courses, and there were some imaginative assessment schemes as well. It had been decreed nationally that a CSE grade 1 was the equivalent of an O level pass. Unfortunately, many employers – and even some universities – refused to accept this equivalence. Apart from the fact that there is an important lesson there for those who are today trying to establish the 'value' of GNVQs by making statements rather than producing evidence, this meant that the great majority of school leavers were going into the world of work with a qualification which was at best not highly regarded and often valueless. For reasons of social justice, apart from practical convenience, this could not be allowed to continue.

The result was hesitant progress towards a new examination at 16+. First came a number of feasibility studies investigating the possibility of examining the full ability range on the same syllabus and the same papers. This turned out to be surprisingly possible in some subjects, but utterly impossible in many more; the crunch came when the physicists demonstrated that an examination paper which would differentiate at all in the top 35% of the ability range was one on which the bottom 40% inevitably and consistently scored 0%. Although this attempt at reform proved abortive, it contributed to the development of GCSE, the first major reform of the examination structure of England and Wales since 1950.

Despite the best efforts of all concerned and mechanisms such as gradient of difficulty and differentiated papers, there is to my mind no doubt that the GCSE is a much less good preparation than O level for academic work post-16. However, at the time when GCSE was introduced only a minority of those who took it went on to any formal post-16 education, and GCSE was clearly a fairer *school leaving* examination than O level – and that was the purpose which it was primarily designed to serve. Its aim was to allow candidates to demonstrate what they knew and could do, not to catch them out in ignorance, and it used a range of assessment techniques including course work which gave everyone a better chance of giving a good account of themselves. For that reason the reform was to be welcomed, for all its faults. GCSE was also, in its grading system, important as the first hesitant step away from an unspoken principle which had informed much of the country's approach to education for at least a century: selection by failure. Apart from social pressures for a more positive approach, it was and is vital that all those involved in any form of education should receive recognition for what they have achieved, however little, not be kicked in the teeth after years of honest, even if relatively ineffectual, study. The arguments for this are so obvious that they do not need restating, but the point still needs to be made while we have a system which allows a student to spend two years on an A level course and end up with a U grade: it beggars belief that anyone could have achieved absolutely nothing during that time.

So, perhaps surprisingly, perhaps not, because there was the will reforms were made. The GCSE was introduced mainly for social and pragmatic rather than educational reasons, but it was a reform which was justified at the time. However, one central aim of that reform, to offer a fair and respected school leaving certificate, has been overtaken by events in that it is now correctly our national objective that everyone should continue in some form of education or training at least until the age of 18, not stop at 16. It follows that the main reason for replacing the failed CSEs, and with them inevitably O levels, with the GCSE no longer applies and the rationale for the very existence of GCSEs is called into question. This is a point which I shall return to later.

The recent past has also seen the introduction of AS levels as vertical 'half' A levels, and of GNVQs. The first, a somewhat timorous move towards breadth post-16, was doomed by official insistence that the examination of half subjects must be at full A level standard; that the AS was misconceived is demonstrated by the failure of the examination to establish itself, but it was at least a try. GNVQs are a totally new concept, and their place is properly discussed in the next section.

Perhaps more important than these changes was the introduction and development of the National Curriculum. This was a strange process. It started with what must have been one of the most ill-thought-out and hastily produced documents to be launched on an unsuspecting world, and was then developed into a very detailed and prescriptive scheme. Since its inception it has undergone numerous modifications, the most important of which stemmed from Sir Ron Dearing's first major review in the field of education. I recognise the reasons which led to the imposition of a National Curriculum while regretting its prescriptive nature, and equally accept that it is here to stay. All that I would say at this stage is that I deplore the misuse of the English language which permeates all discussion in this area where the term 'entitlement' is used as a covert equivalent for 'compulsion'. In any correct use of words, if pupils are 'entitled' to something it must be *made available* to them, but it does not follow that they must do it. Let educational debate be conducted in clear terms, not through weasel words designed to comfort and mislead – and let us avoid the congestion which is, at least in part, a result of 'entitlement' being misinterpreted as 'compulsion'.

The Golden Age?

I now propose to stick my neck out as never before, or at least never since I wrote a thesis on a subject which no-one else knew anything about; I shall aim to give one person's answer to the question: "What do we want for the future?" Two preliminary points. First, as is clear from what I have said already, my life has been spent in what is termed the 'academic' world; nonetheless, in what follows I shall attempt to look to the future not solely of the so-called academic side but of our provision for all those who are in our charge and in whose hands in due course our future will lie. Secondly, while I shall hope to articulate some sort of vision, visions totally disconnected from practicalities are destined to be still-born; I shall therefore look at practical structures as well as what I personally would like to see in terms of provision for the next generations.

First, the curriculum up to 16. It is a good moment to take stock since QCA are starting a major review. I doubt if many of us would argue with the general provisions of Key Stages One to Three, particularly if the review gives appropriate weight to the current 'back-to-basics' moves in literacy and basic mathematics for the early years. The curriculum is crowded, but possible. I would like to see provision for the study of a Modern Language at some point in Key Stage Two because it is self-evident that as many as possible should have a grounding in at least one language other than English, and pupils pick up languages faster and more easily when they are young. It is simple to recommend this, but harder to see where the time to implement the idea is to be found.

There are, however, issues to be addressed. Cross-curricular themes were much beloved of the National Curriculum Council in the early days of the National Curriculum. Many were admirable, but there was little guidance on how to deliver them, and they have been more honoured than delivered. Let us be honest, and either find explicit time provision for them or scrap them. Let us also look again at the massively complex subject guidance documents; the current ones are so full that many sane teachers are driven to the conclusion that it is impossible to deliver what is recommended in less than twice the time allocation which they have. Further, such detailed guidance can stifle the innovation and spontaneity which are essential to stimulating and lively teaching. By all means let there be guidance for those who wish for it or need it, but let us have brief summaries of what should be covered in each Key Stage, and let us make it clear that teachers are free to follow either detailed supporting guidance documents or to choose their own materials and their own mode of delivery if they so wish. Thirdly, let us look again at the content of each stage in each subject to see whether and where each one is overloaded. At the moment, there is very little room for flexibility or for those constructive digressions which are the life-blood of good teaching and excite just that intellectual curiosity which it must surely be our aim to awaken in as many of our pupils as possible. Prescription stultifies the gifted teacher and is in danger of depriving our pupils of just that stimulation which they need and deserve.

Key Stage testing is another area which needs reconsideration. I cannot imagine a well-run school or department where there is not regular testing and where the results of the current cumbersome national testing regime tell teachers or parents anything which they do not know already – but I am assured that I would have been wrong to say this before testing became mandatory. If that is so, there is a case for testing, but I doubt the need for the present time-consuming battery of tests. Testing should be restricted to English and Mathematics, and consist of brief centrally set tests supported by and balanced with teacher assessment.

I have deliberately confined the above remarks to Key Stages One to Three. There is already a real divide at the age of 14 since that is the point at which an element of choice is allowed even under the National Curriculum, and that is the point at which many HMC schools offer their pupils a wider range of options than is permitted to those in the maintained sector. I believe that this change of approach and its timing are both right and appropriate. From that it follows that, in line with HMC policy of the last few years, the national education system should be thinking, planning and talking about 14-19 as a discrete area of the curriculum. Once this becomes the norm, it will be possible to devise a system based on steadily increasing choice, and a controlled reduction in the number of subjects studied which in its turn will facilitate a measured move from general to more specialised study.

However, it is not just a matter of thinking and planning. As indicated above, since it coincides with the school leaving age, in my view GCSE has outlived its usefulness, and can be positively damaging in that it sends a message that there is something terminal about the examinations which all take at the age of 16, and suggests a 'great divide' at that point. Other countries in the European Union and farther afield do not find it necessary to have a massive public examination at 16; nor ought we if we are serious in our national aspiration that all should stay in education and training for at least another two years after GCSE. If it were abolished, little would be lost except externally validated evidence that pupils have covered a wide curriculum up to that point. Incidentally, GCSE does not *per se* even guarantee that since certification is available in one subject; gone are the days of Matric when the certificate was not awarded except to those who had passed in an approved range and number of subjects.

I do not argue with the need for a broad and balanced curriculum at this stage; I merely point out that this alleged justification for GCSE does not hold water. National Records of Achievement are to be relaunched as Profiles: let us use them to record what has been covered up to 16, and do away with a cumbersome, expensive and time-consuming examination which has outlived its purpose. I would rely on teacher assessment, based on an agreed set of national levels and criteria, to complete this Profile. This may be somewhat radical, and may remove some degree of so-called validity from the records, but if the target is for all to move on to further education and training, how much does that matter? In any case, if we are to put new life into our education system, stimulate it and raise standards of achievement, we must as a country go back to *trusting* teachers. As long as Government will accept nothing they say without 'external validation', their confidence and their perception of the value of what they do will remain low. We now have a Government committed to raising standards and trumpeting the importance of education; let them show their confidence by standing back and showing their trust in the professionals who are actually at the chalk face.

If this proposal were accepted for Key Stage Four, the absence of five weeks of public examinations, perhaps coupled with slightly greater flexibility in designing patterns of options, would open the way to some reduction of pressure in what is recognised, even after Sir Ron Dearing's report, to be an over-crowded two years in which there is not in practice even the flexibility which he claimed to have produced. This will become doubly necessary if it is the wish of the Government, as has been suggested recently, to introduce the study of citizenship and some work-related element into the curriculum of this age-group; currently there is not room. Ideally, the passing of GCSE would lead naturally to the abolition of the concept of Key Stage Four and the subsuming of those two years in a new, seamless 14-19 continuum.

There is a further point. Our national educational system has a curiously schizophrenic approach to qualifications. In their reporting of results, the Government ostensibly assumes that all pupils take GCSE after a two year course and at the age of 16, and all A levels are taken after a further two year course. Yet in the world of Further Education we find people encouraged to pick up qualifications when they are ready to take them and often in sequence rather than all together. What is more, GNVQs are not designed necessarily to be completed in two years – and yet an advanced GNVQ is said to be the equivalent of two A levels. Why should study at this level be widely treated as time-limited for some but not for others? It is essential that we abandon the pretence that any particular qualification is necessarily time-limited or age-related. To do this would be to move back towards the approach which informed so much of what happened early in my life when pupils moved to the next stage when they were ready, not at a certain age. Young people simply do not develop at the same rate, a fact which surely everyone knows, but which seems to be too often disregarded.

Such a change would be unlikely to lead to any acceleration except for a very few really able pupils who would benefit from it because they would be properly stretched, not in danger of being bored. It would also allow those who, for whatever reason, would benefit from a slower and more measured approach to realise their true potential rather than be rushed to relative failure. We must all know of pupils who we believe would have benefited from an intermediate year between GCSEs and the full A level course; that was part of the thinking which lay behind the development of the NEAB's experimental 'Intermediate' levels. I personally know pupils who were forced to take an extra year because they had embarked on a Sixth Form course and then a switch of schools made it inevitable that they should restart their A levels; all of them got far higher grades than anyone would have predicted had they taken their A levels after two years. Let us take at face value the simple phrase '14-19 education' which has been so much used in the last few years, and enter candidates for examinations when they are ready for them; we should do them a considerable service. We should also move a long way towards making it possible to meet those National Targets for Education and Training which currently seem admirable but virtually unattainable unless either standards are significantly relaxed or the system is modified to allow students the time they need to develop their full potential and to achieve the best qualifications of which they are capable.

I recognise, of course, that those who have obtained a number of top grades at the same time will have demonstrated a particular sort of ability, and also a type of academic strength which those who take the same qualifications in sequence will not have proved that they possess. It must be for the users of qualifications to decide how important it is to them that their applicants should have demonstrated this ability and to frame their requirements accordingly. I hope that increasing flexibility will become the norm in many areas, but recognise that this is not likely everywhere. For instance, it seems to me inevitable that most medical schools will continue to prefer candidates who have achieved a raft of good grades all obtained at a single sitting to those who have achieved them in sequence over a number of years. They may well be right granted the nature of the degree course on which those students will embark, but their position sits uncomfortably with the fact that we do not expect our potential doctors to demonstrate their competence in all their various areas of expertise at the same sitting.

Moving on to practical implementation, it is clear that one of Sir Ron Dearing's proposals for 16-19 education is vital, the horizontal AS level which HMC originally recommended in 1990. This, perhaps in a slightly modified form, must be the key building block between GCSEs, as long as they exist, or the equivalent internal assessment should the formal examination fade away, and A levels and other parallel qualifications. If the new AS is properly pitched (in today's terminology) at Year 12 level, and the content is not overloaded, it will perform a range of functions. It will be a sensible next step perhaps around the age of 16 for those who have taken GCSE Mathematics early because they are talented in that field; it will be a useful mid-point qualification in a broader curriculum in Year 12; it will also be a sensible final target at 18 or 19 for those who wish to pursue academic study beyond GCSE but lack either the interest or the ability to achieve a full A level. If properly constructed, the new AS should become a strong incentive to further study for a cohort not attracted by full A levels but who want an academic approach rather than the very different GNVQs or NVQs.

Thus we could have a flexible approach starting from the end of Key Stage Three. Following from that, what structures should we look for in the future Sixth Form? The first, and in many ways the most important, point to make is that we must move away from the rigidly separated 'pathways' of Dearing 2. In my dreams we would even abandon all use of the terms 'academic' and 'vocational' in discussing education and the curriculum. The division is artificial, some subjects termed 'academic' are manifestly vocational, and the words themselves are damaging because they imply what I fear is an ingrained tendency to value the one and discount the other. To re-name GNVQs 'vocational A levels' does not deal with the problem; playing with existing terminology is rarely if ever the way to deal with deep-seated prejudice, however misguided.

From this it follows that what emerges from Dearing 2 must include a coherent framework of qualifications designed to interlock naturally. I do not propose to discuss NVQs in detail since I am not qualified to do so. I limit myself to two points. Since they are strictly industry-related, that is a link which must not be lost in the move towards the centralisation of Boards. Secondly, it is vital that there should be central as well as local monitoring of standards to ensure that qualifications described as 'at level 3' should make demands appropriate to that level in order to be credible and accepted. While I see possible interlocks between GNVQs and A levels, I cannot see any similar links with NVQs. Hence, it seems that whatever structure is adopted as a result of Dearing 2, NVQs are likely to remain effectively 'separate' even in the probably rare cases of students taking them in parallel with other qualifications.

Disregarding any political imperative, I am sure that the A level approach must be retained as one option for the future even if the name 'A level' were to be changed; A levels are uniquely appropriate courses for some students, notably those who have a genuine bent towards the academic. They provide a stimulus and a taste of in-depth study and scholarship which students will not meet elsewhere. Equally, the new horizontal AS should provide a 'half-way house' which will be attractive in itself, a sufficient achievement for a proportion of those who take it and a useful stepping stone for many on the way to the full A level.

The Modular approach is spreading, and it seems to me inevitable that all A levels will be constructed on a modular or unit basis in the nearish future, though I regard it as important that the option of taking all modules together at the end of the course and therefore in a linear fashion should remain available. The linear approach remains much the most suitable assessment vehicle for some subjects. The modular approach has considerable benefits in many subjects in terms of student motivation, in its inherent flexibility and because it can genuinely enhance performance and achievement. Syllabuses constructed on a modular basis combined with the new AS levels should provide a way of broadening the 16-19 curriculum and produce the possibility of links between what are at present separate 'pathways', A levels and GNVQs.

A levels are now taken by over 30% of the population, and for many candidates the demands are too abstract and, despite changes to syllabuses and the format of examinations, too great. The Dearing review of 16-19 education also argued that the current three A level curriculum is too narrow and an inappropriate education for today – and this conclusion echoed a general consensus that there should be provision for greater breadth in post-16 education. It is important, before taking this discussion further, to underline the differing ways in which depth can be achieved. At one end of the spectrum, a well designed three A level course which is taught imaginatively, explores subjects widely and in depth and includes differing approaches to learning can in itself be a broad education – certainly much broader than any list of three subjects would imply. If such a course is complemented by proper provision of other subjects and some form of general studies, at least adequate depth is there; witness the reality of my own education which many today would superficially regard as unacceptably narrow. Any provision for the future should preserve the breadth-through-depth option, even if only for a very few, as long as there is the proper complementary and broadening element in the total curriculum undertaken. It is worth remembering that many years ago HMC agreed that a quarter of any Sixth Form timetable should be allocated to subjects other than A levels; we are thus committed – at least in theory – to a reasonably broad curriculum even under the current system.

For many, however, to study three subjects is to do too few. For really able students with wide interests there is a strong case for crossing the Arts/Science divide, and also for taking at least one foreign language to a high level in addition to studying other subjects in depth. Many others do not wish to specialise as we have traditionally done in this country, and for them it is wrong to do so; they too need to be able to take a wider curriculum. It follows that if we are to provide for the varied needs and interests of the whole spectrum, flexibility must be the key, and the provision of appropriate structures and courses is the essential and only way of providing that flexibility.

Also relevant to any discussion of breadth is our current sequence of options which entails a sudden drop from eight to ten subjects taken for the GCSE to three at A level. This is surely too dramatic a step in itself, and is all the worse because GCSEs do not give anything like as good a taste of what A level study in a subject is like as O levels did; therefore pupils find it much harder to make informed choices at 16. Hence the strong case for a more measured taper between 14 and 18. If it were possible to take five or even perhaps six subjects for 12 months after taking eight to ten GCSEs, and then to choose to continue with two or perhaps for the very bright three to the full A level standard, the process would be more measured and choices more soundly based on experience.

A mechanism which will enable us to produce such a taper exists in the new AS levels as long as their content is pitched at the right level. The work done by the Examination Boards under the guidance of SCAA in the immediate aftermath of Dearing 2 took his recommendation at face value and therefore put half the content of an A level into the proposed new AS levels. Even if the new AS were examined at the appropriate level for Year 12, under the current draft proposals the weight of content would make it impossible to cover even five AS levels in the time available in Year 12, and in many combinations three would be the maximum. The opportunity for broadening would be lost. The content of the new AS must therefore be reduced from what has been currently planned. This does not mean that all the work that has been done will have been in vain as long as a simple decision is taken: the AS should be defined as the first two modules of the full A level, not the first three. This should make it possible for able pupils to follow the programme outlined in the last paragraph; they would achieve both the breadth offered by perhaps five subjects in Year 12, and in the following year achieve full A level depth in some of those subjects. The less able might well take two years over two of their AS levels and only take one of the others through to the full A level, and for some students a four or five AS level course taken over more than one year would be a full and adequate curriculum. Thus there would be on the so-called 'academic' side adequate provision for differing interests and ability levels, achievable targets for all and, as long as module outcomes were appropriately certificated, reward for everything achieved.

Any development along these lines must be linked to GNVQs. The proposal for a six unit 'half' GNVQ is an important step forward in that it produces a qualificaton parallel to one A level, but if we are to get away from rigidly separate 'pathways' it will be necessary to go further. Credible parity between modules or units within A level courses and components of GNVQs must be demonstrated. Once that is done and parity of esteem follows, it is essential that there should be cross-recognition of modules/units so that those studying for A levels are able where appropriate to take a module or two drawn from a cognate GNVQ and *vice versa*. Obvious examples would be a Mathematics module from A level in an appropriate GNVQ or a module from GNVQ Engineering which could fit well into a Physics A level course; both could enrich the course in question for the right candidates. If this is to happen, modules must be of the same length and value, and fully recognised by each side.

However, there are other issues to be resolved. The most important mechanical problem is that all GNVQ outcomes are deemed to be at the same level, and therefore at full A level standard. Thus it would, as things stand, be hard to integrate them directly into the new AS levels which are to be examined at Year 12 level; this is surely something which can be overcome by careful planning. A more deep-seated problem is to persuade each side to accept the other's units or modules as of parallel value. This, though, is just the tip of the iceberg. Sooner rather than later the issue of over-all parity must be tackled if GNVQs are to flourish as a genuine alternative to A levels. The effort to establish this recognised parity must have a high priority.

This leads on directly to credit accumulation and transfer. If we are to get away from the philosophy of selection by failure, we must recognise and certificate in some way everything which an individual has achieved, and allow him or her to accumulate over time the necessary units to make up a qualification. Further, we must do all we can to facilitate the aggregation of sub-parts, if necessary and appropriate from different qualifications, in order to allow people to achieve a level 3 qualification. The proposal to have one National Certificate implicitly supports this idea in that it pulls all the current differing strands together under one overarching qualification. Mechanisms for credit accumulation and transfer should be devised to make this work. I do not underestimate the difficulties which lie ahead, but this must be our target. If it can be achieved, one vital step will also have been taken towards genuine parity of esteem between GNVQ and A level. That, I repeat, we must achieve if GNVQs are to succeed – and succeed they must in the national interest; we cannot afford another CSE-type debacle.

A flexible approach such as this will also greatly assist adult returners. If life-long learning is to be anything more than a hollow catch phrase, whatever is devised in the aftermath of Dearing 2 must cater for them and recognise that a large number of those doing what are in schools 'post-16' qualifications are in fact in work or have family responsibilities, and cannot possibly give the sort of time or commitment which is inherent in a full-time Advanced GNVQ or two/three A level course. Time is essential for them – and scarce – and credit accumulation their most natural route to success.

So what structures should we adopt for the future? Having had fairly extensive experience of education in the USA, and with some knowledge of France, I would not adopt either of their systems here; as has been said recently, there is a real danger in transplanting another country's solutions to England and Wales where so much of the context is radically different. Further, I would oppose the imposition of any mandatory curriculum for all in this country because I believe that as students approach university and college their needs and interests are naturally becoming so different that they must be allowed a significant measure of freedom (under appropriate guidance) to follow those interests. Sufficient restraints on random choice are already imposed by entry requirements to degree and similar courses; anything further would be damaging. What is more, students must be free to choose between a significant degree of specialisation and a broader curriculum.

I admire the International Baccalaureate for the right pupils who wish to follow that particular course, but the structure is too restrictive for many. There are areas where I would disagree with the combinations of subjects which are allowed, and more importantly not allowed, but this is a matter of detail which could be changed. Much more seriously, it is time that we recognised that there are people who are mathematically word-blind and others for whom any modern foreign language is likely or certain to remain an impenetrable mystery for life. It follows that, while accepting the value of these subjects for many, I would oppose strongly any attempt to impose Mathematics (a very different thing from practical numeracy) or a modern Foreign Language *for all* in the 16-19 age-group. To do this cannot be right when we are considering the future structure of education for a wide spectrum of ability, and may well be wrong even when we are looking at that for the most able.

For reasons which must by now be clear, I would be equally opposed to any subject-specific requirements for anyone post-16, even if generalised to the level of making all students cross the Arts/Sciences divide. Such a mixed curriculum would be, and is, right for many, and it could well be right to encourage such diversity of subject choice by giving students who have followed such a course preferential treatment in the competition for university places and in recruitment for employment, but to impose it on all would be wrong and damaging for some of our ablest. Such a requirement would also make life even harder for weaker students, and would be well nigh impossible to enforce for adults taking qualifications in sequence over a period.

On the other hand, it is obviously in the national interest that all pupils should have basic Key Skills, and I see no problem in incorporating a reasonable level of numeracy, communication and basic IT competence into any programme as long as the demands made can be fulfilled where appropriate through course work done during the main courses of study. Key Skills cannot and should not be delivered solely through free-standing courses requiring significant time allocation and leading to a further heavy burden of assessment.

Now the central question: what, ideally, would I like to see in the future? First, the taper from the age of 14 described above since I believe that it is the right provision and because the mechanics outlined above allow varying patterns within the curriculum. I believe that it is wrong for almost all, perhaps for all, to drop suddenly at the age of 16 to three A level subjects or the GNVQ equivalent (or less), and that a curriculum which provides only that option is not serving either the students or the country well. Equally, I do not believe that Higginson's five subjects would be right for everyone since they would not relate naturally to GNVQs, and they would not provide for the few for whom the option of real specialist work is right as they embark on A levels. One objective of the current round of reforms must be to preserve the possibility of studying at least two subjects to such a depth that students get, at school or its equivalent, a taste of real scholarship, the challenge of meeting and handling demanding ideas in depth, and the intellectual excitement which springs from that.

It is also necessary to leave enough freedom to those guiding pupils to allow them to develop appropriate combinations of courses for each individual. I have argued above that there can be real breadth in a three A level curriculum as long as it is well taught and supported by appropriate complementary studies which are taken seriously. The problem is that, while many schools and colleges use the freedom they have to lay on a total curriculum of this sort constructively and successfully, there are institutions where students study their three A levels and nothing else, whether because of lack of funding or because the individual is allowed, if he or she so wishes, to do only the bare minimum. However, it would be a monstrous misuse of the powers inherent in the recent Education Act, which effectively even though not overtly introduced Key Stage Five, if the Government saw fit to force a particular form of breadth on all because a minority are misusing the freedom they have at the moment; there are other ways of dealing with them. Germane to this is the enormous value of a non-examined component in any post-16 course. Not merely does it take the pressure off students who are already in many cases working very hard, but it leaves room both for constructive digression and for those teaching to release interesting – even arcane – bees from their bonnets and give them a little exercise; such a process can be equally beneficial for the teacher and the taught.

For similar reasons I would also oppose any proposal to extend the number of taught hours in the week. The comparison between the notional 15 or 16 hours of a three A level course and the 25 or so hours spent in the classroom by the average French student is deeply misleading. To the A level course should be added perhaps another five hours for non-examined teaching, general studies *etc*, to say nothing of the amount of time spent by many of our pupils on games, drama, music and a wide variety of clubs and societies, none of which feature in the French system. In addition to that, it is assumed by those constructing current syllabuses that a student on a three A level course will do about 20 hours a week of private study – three hours a night during the week and five at the week-end. While this is probably a touch optimistic in most cases, these students do do a lot of work other than in the class-room, particularly the increasing number whose chosen subjects include a significant element of coursework. Any mandatory increase in taught time in order to require everyone to do a larger number of subjects could only result in the loss of so much which is of inestimable value in what good schools offer at the moment. The paradoxical effect of such a decision would be that many of our students would end up with a narrower education and be the poorer for the change.

British education has for long had a tradition of specialisation which has not served us anywhere near as badly as some would maintain today. Other countries have gone for breadth and left any real scholarship to degree level, often to second degrees. We should lose something important in 16-19 education if we went down that road. We should also face increasing demands for four-year degree courses, demands which may surface anyway if the 16-19 curriculum is broadened. I do not believe that such demands would be justified because there is at the moment some demonstrable slack at the overlap between A levels and degree courses, but I suspect that they will come. In some ways even more important, the country would lose the enormous benefit we gain from producing PhDs at the age of 24 or 25 who move into front line research at a time when their brains are at their most fertile and sharp, and they have more years of effective research ahead of them than their contemporaries elsewhere.

It follows from all that I have argued above that I do not want to see any particular combination of subjects or any 'core curriculum' post 16 and do not believe that one should be imposed, though I would be content with a requirement to deliver the right sort of Key Skills competence required by universities and employers. Breadth is admirable for some, depth for others, and a combination of the two for many. Equally, a mix of academic and vocational elements must be right in future for yet another group. Of course as many as possible should continue to study a foreign language or take up a new one post-16, but this cannot be for everyone. I repeat: the answer must lie in flexible structures, allied to effective pastoral guidance at institutional level, which will allow varied provision so that the differing needs and aspirations of very different students can all be met.

At a deeper and more important level, the key thing which we must do is to introduce those in our care to the excitement and challenge of new ideas – and that applies at all levels and in all types of course. We must offer them a sensible and balanced choice between breadth and depth, and we must not produce an examination-ridden system which takes all the fun out of learning. There was a marvellous zest about the Renaissance, perhaps only matched once before in fifth century Athens, and a shadow of that fervour and excitement still lingers here and there today. Let us fan it to life again; let whatever structure we produce, mechanistic as it must be at a certain level, be subservient to that aim.

I know of no way to achieve this except by freeing our teachers so that they can excel as they should. I am sure that over-obsession with examinations and over-crowded, prescriptive curricula are death to scholarship and to real success.

Chapter 2

An alternative curriculum

Tommy Cookson
Headmaster, Sevenoaks School

Independent schools have lost their independence. Of course, they can hire whom they like, can run their own finances, build their own buildings, choose their own governors. But in the most important educational matter, the curriculum, they have surrendered control to others. If you look at the curricula of almost all schools, you see the same subjects, the same system, the same examinations – indeed, it is the examinations which determine the subjects and the system.

This is unsatisfactory. The most important justification for an independent system is that it should take risks and explore new ideas, as well as hang onto good things which have ceased to be fashionable. The schools which belong to the HMC are the most privileged in the world: they have able pupils, highly motivated parents, intelligent teachers; some of them have nice buildings and grounds and quite a few have cash in the bank. But despite all these advantages they have lost confidence in themselves. Instead of devoting their time to the pioneering work for which they ought to be uniquely qualified, they are spending time on marketing, PR, and on ensuring they do well in the league tables of examination results.

The league tables will not do the independent schools any good in the long term. They have led to obsessive concern with examinations, to the point where a pupil's academic education is now identified solely with his or her success in GCSE and A level; and a school's quality is seen very largely as reflected by its place in the league tables. The effect on the ablest pupils, to whom the examinations offer too little challenge and an ever-narrowing scope, is obvious. There is apparently nothing to be gained by reading widely, or by learning subjects which do not fit in to a conventional pattern. After the age of 16, there is little incentive for scientists to learn to write English, to read novels or philosophy, to debate or understand political issues, to learn to speak, read and understand to a high level at least one modern foreign language in a shrinking world, to absorb another culture besides their own; students of English or History need not study Mathematics post-16, or continue with Science. English pupils are conditioned, as soon as they join secondary school, by a culture of giving up subjects they do not like or find difficult. In this they are encouraged by their teachers who advise them to do congenial subjects, no matter how narrow the cluster of A levels they take, and who hunt around for syllabuses and boards likely to offer the least difficulty and to yield the best results. In their desire to show up well in the league tables, independent schools are now no better than those Third World countries which burn down forests in order to plant cash crops. Our Sixth Forms are now planting oil-seed rape to be harvested next June, or greenhouse cabbages harvested in modules every three months.

This approach to education is spurious and its evaluation by league tables insulting. But our teachers can hardly be blamed. Heads who have once been Heads of Departments know that HoDs have the hardest job of the lot. Heads and Housemasters can have their performance evaluated in many ways; but the Head of Department faces annually a trial by exam results. Innovation in such circumstances becomes risky. Self-development in terms of reading more widely, especially beyond one's own subject, is difficult. For HoDs to develop a broad view of education is, in practice,

Tommy Cookson went to Winchester and then to Balliol College, Oxford. He has taught in Germany, America, Manchester Grammar School and Winchester College, where he was Head of English and later a Housemaster. After six years as Head of King Edward VI School, Southampton, he is now Headmaster of Sevenoaks School.

unlikely. They and their departments see it as their duty to do better what they already do, to request better resources and more time. Curriculum change is painful, and the hardest task for a Head is to bring it about. Most Heads leave it alone: it is not a frequent topic of discussion at inter-school meetings. Indeed such change is seen as something altogether too big to discuss, even by an influential body of independent schools.

This would not matter so much if the National Curriculum, the GCSE and the A levels and GNVQs were more interesting, more flexible, attuned to the abilities of more able pupils and their needs in the world of the future. But able pupils are given little to spur them on between the ages of 13 and 16. In most subjects they spend three years to GCSE, when two years would be enough. To keep them occupied they are given coursework, and the promise of a grade called A*, not as a reward for doing more challenging work, but simply for gaining higher marks. Top universities demand A* at GCSE. It is therefore too risky to take GCSE early and go on to more interesting and challenging work; and the middle parts of many of our schools are threatened by intellectual sagging and low expectations. The underperformance of boys at GCSE may be due as much to the lack of urgency as to the alleged slowness of their development. Or, of course, they may be very bored. Boys are, in general, less willing to please.

After GCSE comes A level, the main shortcomings of which are its absence of prescribed balance and its encouragement of an unnecessarily high degree of specialisation at an age where such a degree of specialisation is inappropriate. For instance, few other education systems in the world allow their pupils to cease writing and reading their own language before they have discovered its delights, its complexities, its taxing disciplines of clarity and coherence. No other system would begin to require pupils to follow a course of study which did not offer to their imaginations the treasures of its literature, especially if its literature is so rich. In a world which is undergoing rapid scientific change and where distances are rapidly shrinking, the educated man or woman should at least be able to follow the progress of science and have more than a tourist's view of someone else's language and culture. For pupils to be able to jettison Science and Modern Languages so early is wrong. But our system suits the universities, who want a four-year course but cannot have it and so insist that our Sixth Forms supply the omission.

A level has already become discredited because it is perceived to have got easier. Like so much else in education, it is a victim of an upwardly mobile society hungry for qualifications, whose acquisition has reduced examinations not so much to tests of knowledge, understanding, independence of thought, clarity of expression and so on, but more to rites of passage where the marks matter most. A new generation asks not what education is for but more vociferously than ever what certificates it can provide.

Independent schools have played the league tables game because in the short term they have done very well out of it. With access to the best of everything they have enjoyed the publicity they have got from coming top, have enjoyed vying with their rivals and have done little to undeceive the customers who think league tables matter more than anything else. But the price has been appallingly high. It has produced a restricted curriculum and teaching methods designed to ensure that the syllabus is covered in the minutest detail, so that little is left to chance. Lecturing and spoonfeeding stifle exploration and independent thinking. Teachers become more and more specialised and, from year to year, give not only the same exam lessons, but more and more of them as non-examined studies get pushed to the curricular margins. Teachers know little of what their colleagues in other subjects are doing and, therefore, neglect opportunities for fruitful collaboration.

They seldom have a panoramic view of the whole curriculum and exercise little influence on the curriculum because others are making decisions about what it is important to know. They are not being challenged and feel, long before retirement, the stress that is the result of hard work without very much interest in it. The system also produces able pupils who sense a lack of intellectual challenge but who, like their teachers, feel the weight of high school-and-parent expectations – and who therefore resist the challenges of what is exciting because of the already-existing burden of what is not exciting. No wonder universities complain that, as results get better each year, so their undergraduates know less; no wonder employers discover that their employees cannot write English or do simple arithmetic.

Schools have paid too much attention to results because that is the only part of their business which is measurable. There are no prizes for having excellent systems of pastoral care, even though the pressures on young people have increased, the higher incidence of divorce and separation has left them with less support, and the dangers of eating disorders and legal and illegal drugs have left them more vulnerable. There are no prizes for high standards in the many extra-curricular activities, even though the skills they teach (such as teamwork, the ability to manage oneself and other people) have greater importance in later life than success in examinations. There are certainly no prizes for what lies at the heart of a successful school – the willingness of individuals to behave decently, unselfishly and sensitively in their relationships or through service to the community.

A system of crude measurement through examinations is all we have to measure ourselves by, and we have lost control of it. Our pupils will be measured only in these terms; and soon we will be seen as 'successful' only if we have 'added value' to our pupils in terms of the examination grades they score compared with their 'ability'. The very term 'added value' is borrowed from Marxist economics to describe the value imparted by workmen upon raw materials through an industrial process.

But to this language have we inevitably come in a system designed and sanctified by politicians with the aim of increasing the Gross National Product, not of cultivating its citizens. That is perhaps why our curriculum has been slanted towards subjects which are considered useful, in the narrow sense of marketable; the Sciences and Technology occupy a larger space in the National Curriculum than they should, especially when an important subject like History is not only a non-compulsory constituent of Key Stage 4, but is now given less time in primary schools; and computers devour the development budget, although their day-to-day educational uses beyond word-processing, number-crunching and information gathering have yet to be properly incorporated. Relevance and usefulness sit oddly with Cardinal Newman's thoughtful statement of the deeper aims of education:

"...knowledge is not a mere extrinsic or accidental advantage, which is ours today and another's tomorrow, which may be got up from a book, and easily forgotten again, which we can command or communicate at our pleasure, which we can borrow for the occasion, carry about in our hand, and take into the market; it is an acquired illumination, it is a habit, a personal possession, and an inward endowment. And this is the reason why it is more correct, as well as more usual, to speak of a university as a place of education, than of instruction, though, where knowledge is concerned, instruction would at first sight have seemed the more appropriate word. We are instructed, for instance, in manual exercises, in the fine and useful arts, in trades, and in ways of business; for these are methods, which have little or no effect upon the mind itself... But education is a higher word; it implies an action on our mental nature, and the formation of a character. When, then, we speak of the communication of knowledge as being Education, we thereby really imply that that knowledge is a state or condition of mind; and since cultivation of mind is surely worth seeking for its own sake, we are thus brought once more to the conclusion ... that there is a knowledge, which is desirable though nothing come of it, as being of itself a treasure, and a sufficient remuneration for years of labour." (*The Idea of a University*, Discourse V, Section 6)

The time has come for schools to reassert their ownership of the curriculum in the long-term interests of the minds and characters of their pupils, not the short-term interests of political parties or even the former Head of the Post Office. This is not to imply that education has no useful function; but that the effect of a good education is lifelong benefit, the 'acquired illumination' and the 'inward endowment' described by Newman. Schools should ask themselves not "What's in the syllabus?" but what they would like their pupils to know. The fact that this is not an easy task does not mean it should be shelved. Different schools will provide a different emphasis, which is as it should be: the attempt to achieve a National Curriculum to which all parties sign up is a recipe for mindless orthodoxy. One school could place greater emphasis on Mathematics, another on Science, another on Languages, another on Literature, another on Music, another on Latin and Greek, another on Art and Design. But each would probably see itself as passing on an aspect of Western European culture, beginning with British culture (especially the English Language) and History, and branching out into European and World history, culture and ideas.

At Sevenoaks there is a large Sixth Form, approximately half of which takes the International Baccalaureate. Here is a recent – and judging by its rapidly growing popularity, successful – attempt to allow choice at the same time as insisting that important areas of study should not be ignored. In the IB it is compulsory to study both your own language, through its literature, and the literature of other countries;

a modern foreign language; a Humanity, including Philosophy; a Science; Mathematics; one other subject of your choice. Of these six, you can choose which three to take at Higher and which three at Subsidiary Level. You score the same number of points for each (7 for excellent, down to 1 for rudimentary) whether you take them at Higher or Subsidiary Level. In addition, you have to write an Extended Essay of 4000 words on an approved subject of your choice; you have to take the Theory of Knowledge course which aims through discussion to make you see what is prejudice and what is knowledge. Finally, you must do a certain number of hours of Community Service.

The popularity of the IB worldwide and at Sevenoaks is demonstrated by the fact that it is growing at a steady rate of 10% a year. The exam reinforces our emphasis on internationalism through the compulsory Modern Foreign Language, the emphasis on World Literature, and the Theory of Knowledge course; it is demanding; it considers certain subjects of such importance that it does not allow pupils to drop them; it keeps teachers fresh through obliging them to develop other aspects of study than A level and through the supervision of the Extended Essay and the teaching of Theory of Knowledge.

I am surprised that more independent schools have not adopted the IB or some sort of Baccalaureate system. The IB was founded in Geneva in the 1960s and has had 30 years to sort itself out. It is recognised by the leading universities who value the breadth and the commitment that its candidates show. Because it requires study of three subjects at Higher Level, it cannot be accused of lacking the depth of A level; and because it requires so much more than three Higher Level subjects it constitutes a serious and intelligent commitment to breadth. A crucial feature is the need for candidates to explore further subjects they may not be very good at (as my tutor at Oxford used to say, "It keeps your wounds open.").

We should be exploring a similar system. We should not wait for the DfEE to pronounce. Independent schools have marked time because they have for many years been waiting for reforms which have been promised, modified, delayed or cancelled. What we have got are Modular A levels but no apparent insistence that they should emphasise breadth. These will not encourage wider reading or extra-curricular activities, because of the frequency of the sittings. The IB has no plans to follow A level down the modular route.

Independent status is a privilege and carries with it a responsibility to think and act independently in pursuit of what is worthwhile in the new and what is best in the old. Failure to establish our own educational agenda will ultimately call into question the need for an independent sector. The very survival of our schools will be threatened if we fail to demonstrate to an increasingly critical and perceptive generation of parents that our product is, to put it bluntly, worth the money.

We have a duty to aim higher than the top of the league tables. Independent schools must regain their independence.

Chapter 3

Restarting the conversation: Science in the curriculum

Graham Able
Master, Dulwich College

Whenever I have mentioned my subject, Chemistry, at a cocktail party, it has proved a conversation stopper. Why is ignorance of science so widespread and so socially acceptable where a similar lack of appreciation of the arts is certainly not?

What do we mean by the word 'science'? What, if anything, is so greatly different about those academic subjects which group under this particular banner as against those referred to as 'arts' or 'social sciences'? The word, science, is derived from Latin and is best translated as 'knowledge'. This perhaps has led to the myth that science is somehow to do with lots and lots of facts. On closer inspection, however, there seems to me to be little difference between a 'scientific' fact and a 'geographical' or 'historical' fact. Yet the perception amongst non-scientists tends very much to be that science peddles dry factual knowledge, whereas the arts and social sciences encourage more open-ended discussion and discursive argument.

The truth is vastly different. The common ground between those subjects which we would normally term sciences is that theories are being developed and hypotheses put forward in all of them to explain observations which can be consistently made under defined and controlled conditions. Our scientific knowledge and understanding moves forward by testing our hypotheses at the limits and redeveloping them. Thus the true progress of science owes more to the philosophy of Karl Popper than it does to the cult of heurism which has inspired many changes in the teaching of sciences – most of them for the better – over the last 30 years. It is good for pupils to discover 'science by experimentation', but we should not forget that all rational experiments and most real progress are preceded by the formulation of hypotheses which the experiments are then designed to test.

If the nature of science is not well understood by non-scientists, the differences between the subjects which traditionally make up the school science curriculum are even less appreciated. From a personal point of view, I am considerably better qualified to teach Greek or Latin than I am Biology; at least I have O levels in the former two subjects, whereas my biological education was restricted to one term on the particularly uninteresting sex life of the King Edward potato. As a chemist, if I had to find a second subject, I would actually be happier teaching either Mathematics or Information Technology than Physics, if only because my knowledge of the latter has become very rusty through lack of practice.

Although teachers of scientific subjects of a more recent vintage are likely to be much better qualified to cross the boundaries of the three traditional school sciences than veterans of my generation, nevertheless most of them will have a particular interest and special expertise in one subject. Of course, there is considerable overlap between molecular biology and Chemistry; similarly the boundaries between physical chemistry and applied physics cannot be sharply defined. This should not prevent non-scientists from understanding, however, that the relationship between Physics and Chemistry is no closer than that between History and Geography or, indeed, between French and Spanish.

Graham Able took up the Mastership of Dulwich College on 1 January 1997. After taking a degree in Natural Sciences at Cambridge, he taught Chemistry for 14 years at Sutton Valence. He came to the College following five years as Second Master at Barnard Castle and nine years as Headmaster of Hampton School. He is Chairman of the Academic Policy Sub-Committee from September 1998.

Why then have we moved to a curriculum which in most schools groups the three traditional sciences together to the end of Key Stage 4? The first reason is that there is a shortage of science teachers. This shortage is currently most acute for physicists and least acute for biologists. Secondly, there was a realisation, when the National Curriculum was being developed, that it was wrong for pupils to opt out of any of the sciences at an early stage. Increasingly, industry and commerce regarded a broad scientific base as being desirable in those people it was looking to employ. This led to the very reasonable conclusion that all students should study at least elements of all three major sciences to the end of Key Stage 4.

Given both the perceived and actual difficulties, particularly for the less academically inclined, with regard to parts of the traditional Chemistry and Physics O level syllabuses, given the over-crowded nature of the curriculum and given the shortage of specialist science teachers, the 'dual award' route had – and still has – much to commend it. Certainly as a vehicle for 'science for all' and as a programme of scientific education scheduled to finish at 16, the 'dual award' science at GCSE is probably the best option available, and it can be taught 'separately' by three individual subject specialists in a co-ordinated approach. Equally, it is possible for the whole syllabus to be delivered as an integrated package if this is deemed desirable and if the necessary staff expertise is available. Whilst this latter approach may have the attraction of greater coherence, at least to non-scientific senior colleagues, there is a real danger that the subject specialism of the teacher will make delivery uneven across the three disciplines.

But is there a conflict between 'science for all' and a good basis for those who wish to commit themselves to further study in Physics, Chemistry and/or Biology? For such people, the inevitable dilution of merging three subjects into two, often leading to the omission of the more challenging and interesting topics, is not the best platform for further scientific education. It is interesting, therefore, that the majority of HMC and GSA schools have made provision for the teaching of the three separate sciences in Key Stage 4, as well as providing dual-award courses for those less scientifically inclined. This would seem to have been successful in most cases and to be educationally desirable. Funding and more restrictive National Curriculum requirements have precluded such a dual approach in most maintained sector schools, although it is noticeable that many of the traditional grammar schools have managed to keep the separate sciences option at GCSE: it should be noted that many schools manage to teach each of the three separate sciences on three-quarters of the time normally allocated to a GCSE subject in years 10 and 11. This is partly a recognition that some common material exists in the syllabuses but is more a necessary consequence of our crowded curriculum. This does mean that such schools are able to deliver the three separate subjects with only marginally more contact time than that recommended for 'dual award' courses.

As a chemist myself, I know that this necessitates very tight schemes of work, but it can be done successfully and to the advantage, many would argue, of more able pupils. One should not, however, make too big an issue of the basis for A level study. All pupils today come across science at an early stage in their education. In my own case, I did no science at all until two years before O level, and this was not at all unusual in the late 1950s and early 1960s. Nor did such a short exposure prevent us either from choosing or succeeding on A level science courses.

The evolution of science education in schools has been considerable over the past 40 years. In the 1950s, few schools taught any meaningful science before the age of 14. On the old O level system of 16-plus examinations, various scientific options evolved. There were separate examinations in Physics, Chemistry and Biology, but it was comparatively rare, certainly until 30 years ago, for students to take all three subjects at this level. There was also the option of combination examinations in either physics with chemistry (a single O level) or general science. The latter was never regarded as adequate preparation for A level in any of the three separate subjects and tended to be taken by those who had made a decision at 14 against furthering their scientific horizons beyond O level. Indeed in many distinguished schools at that time, there was still a tradition for choosing eventual specialisations as early as 14 or 15. The filtering down of science teaching to what we now regard as the Key Stage 3 age range occurred during the 1960s, but it was not until more recent times that any systematic approach to science was made in the primary years.

The advent of GCSE and the National Curriculum had a radical effect on science education, especially in the 14 to 16 age range. The old double O level in integrated science had been markedly less popular than the three separate subjects, but the restraints of the initial, very prescriptive National Curriculum and the move towards 'balanced science for all' meant that the GCSE examination system heralded a rapid and numerically overwhelming change from separate subject certification to 'dual award science'. It is interesting to speculate whether this change has been in itself largely, or even partially, responsible for the subsequent move away from science subjects (and particularly Physics and Chemistry) at A level. It would seem from research which I carried out with others in the early 1990s that those schools which retained the three single subject entries at GCSE for at least the majority of their pupils had a much better up-take of the three sciences in the Sixth Form than those schools which went entirely the dual award route.

There were other factors, however, which also conspired against the take up of science in the Sixth Form, most noticeably the perceived degree of difficulty of Mathematics and the two physical sciences compared to other subjects. This perceived additional difficulty would appear from Professor Carol Fitz-Gibbon's research to be very real and may even have led some schools with an eye on league tables to steer their less gifted pupils away from Physics and Chemistry. A further factor was undoubtedly the publicity given at various stages during the 1970s and 1980s to the lack of employment opportunity in the sciences. This trend has recently been reversed, not by the greater availability and reward for scientific employment, but by the increasing tendency of merchant banks, large accountancy firms and other City employers to show a distinct liking for those with scientific and engineering first degrees. This has apparently still not filtered down to those entering post-GCSE education, however, because the take-up in scientific subjects, especially the physical sciences, had remained in decline until a slight incremental rise last year. It is also evident that places on scientific and engineering degree courses are still less fully subscribed than those in the arts and social sciences. Even those with scientific A levels often prefer degree courses where their university time is less fully directed and the path to graduation is perceived to be less onerous.

Looking to the future, how would we see the ideal place of scientific subjects in our school curriculum? I would like to think that the 'science for all' movement is irreversible. In a modern, increasingly scientific and digital age, we surely have a duty to educate all youngsters in the basic tenets of the major scientific subjects. Having said this, however, I hope that an increasing number of schools will give pupils who are scientifically inclined the opportunity to study the three separate subjects to GCSE – or its equivalent stage once this examination becomes an irrelevance, which it must surely do as fewer people leave full-time education at 16-plus. The syllabuses of the separate subjects tend to contain the more demanding elements which are sometimes omitted from dual award science; this is especially so regarding Chemistry.

There would seem to be some evidence that some of our brightest teenagers are so under-challenged by the dual award syllabus that they dismiss sciences as being unworthy of their further study. I feel that some of these would continue with science for longer if they were given more stimulating material post 14. Curriculum time is very tight at this level and one would not wish to reduce options available in the humanities or modern languages, but it may be possible for more schools to consider funding the marginal increase in teaching time required to deliver the separate subjects to the most able pupils.

The other way in which we could encourage more people to keep on an element of science post-GCSE would be to broaden the curriculum at this stage and delay choice for at least another year. Five subjects taken for a year post-GCSE would encourage more to keep at least an element of science going for a further 12 months, and the delayed choice would perhaps even increase the numbers going for the equivalent of a full A level. It seems that the gradual narrowing down post 14, perhaps going from eight or ten subjects to five subjects and then to three for a final year would give a better pattern and allow the critical final choices to be made at a more mature stage. It would be important that the final specialisation could still occur, otherwise there would be an immediate need to add years on to our first degree honours courses in the sciences and engineering.

Much has been written in criticism of the specialisation of the English Sixth Form education, but we should remember that we get people to good first degree level more quickly than any of our western European counterparts. This is an advantage we should throw away only after carefully weighing up the consequences. The delayed choice would give greater breadth post-GCSE, but would still allow the necessary further narrowing down to provide the specialisation which scientists need to embark successfully on degree level work. If such scientists of tomorrow were to study one or two subjects from the arts or social sciences for at least a year post-GCSE, then one hopes that this would help to build a bridge between C P Snow's two cultures.

Similarly, the modular system, properly refined, could – and should – lead to a range of options from 14- to 18-plus. Ideally this would see most, if not all, students doing at least some science which is more advanced than the current GCSEs. A fully modular structure for examinations at 18- plus is now virtually in place. This is not universally favoured in all subjects, but it has generally been welcomed by mathematicians and scientists, and its advantages for curriculum design could be considerable. If the new intermediate award (currently termed AS level) could be redesigned as one-third of the current A level content (*ie* two units of a six-unit A level) then it would be possible to envisage a teaching programme involving five subjects at this level for one year post GCSE, followed by a narrowing down to complete the full A level in two or three subjects in a further year. This would involve only slightly more contact time than is currently the case for a traditional three A level course and would encourage a wider participation in science post GCSE. Such a structure could even create a demand for an 'Intermediate' qualification in science (rather than Chemistry, Physics or Biology) for the committed arts/humanities student to improve his or her scientific literacy.

The crowded nature of the curriculum up to GCSE and the cost of any additional contact teaching time thereafter are factors which must be considered in any new initiatives. The better understanding of the potential – and limitations – of IT in increasing directed learning time without adding to teaching timetables could radically alter the concept of curriculum delivery over the next few years. IT is more widely used in science teaching than in some other subject areas, but for most the computer is still regarded as just another teaching tool or piece of apparatus – an upmarket animated OHP or an experimental 'black box'. These uses are perfectly valid and will doubtless be further refined and extended to the benefit of our teaching, but it is the development of interactive learning programmes which could enable us to deliver an enhanced scientific curriculum without significant additional teaching costs. These programmes will never replace the need for classroom or laboratory teaching, but they should allow additional directed learning opportunities for our pupils.

The continuing debate about moral and health education also has curriculum implications for science. Although there is much health and safety education covered in science at the various key stages, it is not necessarily the right timetable slot for all the issues involved: given that curriculum time is limited, however, it does seem sensible that all institutions should be careful to avoid unnecessary duplications in their teaching programmes. Moral issues will arise naturally in the teaching of any subject, and the sciences provide many opportunities in this area; similarly there are several topics which naturally allow environmental issues to be investigated with more intellectual honesty and rigour than our students will generally find in the media.

My hope for the future? Maybe I will be able to go to a cocktail party in 20 years' time and admit to being a scientist without stopping the conversation: that would be real progress.

Chapter 4

Heading a Science Department

Bryan Collins

Headmaster, Leeds Grammar School

So, you have been appointed Head of Science; congratulations. You have already made considerable progress in your career, in that you must have established yourself as a successful teacher of one or more of the science subjects and you may already have headed a subject section or department. Now you have wider responsibilities and in this chapter we will examine them in the whole school context.

It is therefore appropriate to state what this chapter is and what it is not. It is *not* a detailed work of reference on the technicalities of running a science department; there are other guides to that, in whole, or to aspects of the job. It *is* an attempt to examine the role from the perspective of a Head, one who has the background of having run three science departments and, at the time of writing, still teaches two science subjects.

As Head of Science, the Head will look to you as one of his/her heads of larger and key departments to advise on curricular issues and to ensure successful delivery of one of the three core subject areas of the National Curriculum. The Head will be conscious that your department represents a large capital investment for the school, that it demands on-going improvements, that it is very significant in terms of total staffing cost, and that it also requires a high proportion of the academic expenditure each year to meet its departmental budget. The Head, even if not a scientist, will be aware that there are particular health and safety considerations relating to science departments and will want to be satisfied, through you, that these are given appropriate attention; indeed, he may look to you for advice on broader health and safety issues.

In face of the wide perspective of responsibilities for a significant chunk of the estate, a large slice of the financial cake, real and potential safety issues, and a good deal of operational complexity, it would be tempting to concentrate on these aspects of the role of Head of Science. That would be a mistake; for your primary responsibilities are to *people* – to deliver the curriculum in the most effective possible way to your pupils, via good teaching and learning, and to encourage, support and develop the talents of your departmental staff. What has just been rehearsed is the key role for you as for any other head of department, the role of *management*. The Head will want to take all the other aspects of the job more or less for granted, *but he will*

Bryan Collins was educated at Glyn Grammar School, Epsom, and the universities of London and Bristol. He headed three maintained school science departments, was a curriculum Deputy Head and secured the Headship of his old school in 1977. He was appointed Headmaster of Leeds Grammar School in 1986. He chairs the HMC Junior Schools Working Party.

look to see you developing your effectiveness as a manager.

Most of this chapter will therefore concentrate on the Head of Science as manager in the particular setting of teaching and learning basic science and the separate science subjects. However, the health and safety aspects and the technical aspects of the role must be discharged, so an early survey of the department should be undertaken, remembering that more detailed advice is obtainable elsewhere.

Your survey of the whole department, in association with your staff, will almost certainly have highlighted matters for attention – those health and safety matters for the shorter term (the right fire extinguishers, separate bins for general rubbish and broken glassware); the items for future development (renewing the old greenhouse so that you can propagate your own plant stock, creating a dark room, finding additional storage, refurbishing antiquated laboratories). Hopefully, this working together on tangible everyday matters of teaching science and the things which you *must* do, will have produced an atmosphere for working together on the things which you *should* do. That leads us back to your position, occupying the middle ground between your Head and your departmental staff, your role in general management.

The science curriculum, its delivery, and the quality of pupils' work and learning will need to be kept under constant review. That review needs co-ordination and careful consideration and those criteria demand meetings. There are still departments which try to kid themselves (and sometimes inspecting teams) that because everyone is so matey, and the prep room/coffee room is so small and the senior technician is married to the head of biology, that everything can be done by informal chats at break and meetings would represent imposed bureaucracy.

Your Head is unlikely to be persuaded by such reactions. That does not mean that meetings should be unduly laboured; your colleagues will thank you for making them regular, giving them a short printed agenda to think about in advance, operating a sensible and agreed guillotine, and promptly publishing bullet points only of matters agreed for record and for action. Pass a copy for information to the Head; it will impress and genuinely keep him informed. The Deputy Head/Director of Studies is unlikely to be able to timetable the meetings but that should not deter you from trying.

Consider the position of technicians. If you want to keep them at the level of trolley porters and test-tube washers, exclude them from your deliberations. If you want them to *understand* what is required for demonstrations and class practicals, where these fit into the development of the course, and if you want them to suggest how delivery of the curriculum may be improved, include them in your meetings (another good reason for getting the meetings timetabled if you can). As an aside, if you are not happy with the quality of your technicians and you have the chance for replacements, seriously consider a 'term time plus' basis of appointment, with limited work in school holidays. You lose time for getting certain maintenance work done but you can gain the potential to recruit well qualified mothers, possibly science graduates. The gain in subject expertise may greatly outweigh the loss in total hours. Incidentally, it is not cost-effective to have anyone washing test tubes that cannot be done by pupils at the end of a practical; get industrial grade laboratory glass washers and save precious technician time for more cerebral pursuits.

To return to curriculum planning, your managerial responsibility is to ensure that the science curriculum is thoroughly considered, well delivered and frequently reviewed. If you are Head of Science but not a head of subject you are probably in an ideal position. If, as is more likely, you are also a head of subject you must be careful not so to dominate the subject that less experienced colleagues are not given a chance to develop. You must also acquire the art of balanced judgement so that you give equal consideration to all the subject areas. It is a good principle that all teaching staff should have some responsibility for curriculum development, for evaluation, for assessment, and for curriculum review and revision. Most independent schools teach an integrated science course for the first one of two secondary years before embarking on separate subjects. That introductory course will benefit from input by subject specialists from each of the disciplines, with responsibility for the course revolving over time.

Curriculum planning years ago may have consisted of drafting a paragraph or two outlining topics to be covered in the term. In these times of rapid change (National Curriculum, Key Stage testing, practical assessments for GCSE, modular A levels) that approach will no longer do, if it ever did! The curriculum plan should include schemes of work, and will need specification of:

general aims

specific objectives

topics to cover

relevant demonstrations and class practicals

risk assessments

resources available

possibly scheduled unit tests.

Hopefully you will have inherited some up-to-date IT, hardware and software, in the department. If not, you should make an early bid to get some, although you will undoubtedly have to fit in to general school planning on IT development. Your curriculum planning, utilising IT, will enable you *inter alia*, to:

present the curriculum in a readily understandable way for teachers and technicians

present the curriculum in a suitable form for pupils

make modifications easily

code demonstrations and class practicals to their worksheets, risk assessments and apparatus/reagent requirements

code other resource materials (videos, simulation programmes, CD ROM references)

code relevant revision tests and (for teachers!) the specimen answer sheets.

The use of IT obviously has enormous potential for the more efficient *running* of science departments, enabling linkage of curriculum planning to learning and teaching (the worksheet specifying the practical including risk assessments and apparatus requirements, changeable at the touch of a button in the light of experience today ready for tomorrow's class; the virtual image display of apparatus and reagent location). Few would claim to have done more than lightly touch the keypad so far. As with other aspects of our work, we are more likely to progress our systems in a collaborative atmosphere. IT usage may be enhanced by inter- as well as intra-departmental collaboration.

The exponential growth of IT presents a more fundamental challenge than the organisation of our worksheets and our apparatus. We have the opportunity to re-examine *how children may best learn* and *how we may best use our resources of teacher expertise*. This brings us up against other fundamentals of your role as a manager. Hopefully your early moves in assessing the physical state of the department with your colleagues, your prompt establishment of departmental meetings and your agreements on division of labour regarding running the laboratories, curriculum planning and pupil assessment, will have created a mood for openness to monitoring teachers' teaching and pupils' learning. Science departments are better placed than most subject areas for this in that technicians and colleagues tend from time to time to encroach on one another's teaching space.

We become accustomed to others being in our classes but that will not do as 'observation' if you really want to take your department forward. So, explicitly open up your own teaching and your pupils' learning to your colleagues' observation and assessment; after due process require them to reciprocate. If there is reluctance, get the ball rolling by asking a colleague to observe you teaching a particular topic and to give you critical feedback; ask another to evaluate the learning acquired by named pupils in one of your classes over a particular topic, including an assessment of the increment from one lesson (get them to use HMC lesson observation forms from our OFSTED evaluated scheme; almost all HMC schools will now have one or more trained inspectors experienced with these materials).

Having got the ball rolling, keep it rolling. Your curriculum planning will have established, in the present context, *what* it is you want your pupils to learn. You are now into the much more challenging and open-ended arena of *how* they may best learn. The rapid technical developments of IT and the associated decreasing expense of using it, is presenting the opportunity of moving forward rapidly in facilitating a change of emphasis. The traditional situation represents teachers, as repositories of knowledge, transmitting part of that knowledge to pupils, who thereby learn principally from their teachers. The possibility is before us of pupils operating as increasingly self-directed learners, using a variety of resources (not all IT based); with teachers being there to stimulate, to guide, at times to direct, to be providers of some of the knowledge and, as a result of their experience of the subject and of life, of much of the wisdom.

Observation of a science lesson, against the background of the curriculum the department has planned, should therefore be attempting to answer these questions among others:

What are the pupils supposed to be learning?

What are they learning?

What has a particular individual learned in the lesson?

Has learning been acquired in the most efficient way?

What has been the teacher's role in assisting that learning?

Could the teacher's time have been deployed in a more efficient way?

Relating these considerations to the possibilities opening up by the use of IT:

use of curriculum material on a departmental or school intranet as a source of much of a pupil's coursework, allowing teachers to arrange and monitor individual target setting;

video demonstrations delivered by a multimedia system for some complex and time-consuming processes;

pupil access to practical work instructions (including highlighted risk assessments) to be carried out in the course of his/her sequence of work;

teacher supervision of individual pupils' work via an interactive network;

pupil access to resource material on departmental or school intranet, or via the internet;

extension work for faster/more able pupils;

consolidation exercises for slower /less able pupils;

assessment tasks at key points, capable of being monitored on screen by the teacher and the results placed in departmental records.

The above just trails ideas, some of which are extant in our schools, others of which should develop rapidly. Once a department starts to move down this line of development, the need for a very open approach to collaboration in the management of physical resources and of people becomes increasingly obvious. The possibilities for improving the quality of individual learning and the effectiveness of the science teacher, should also become increasingly obvious, while retaining the best of existing elements such as the lively question and answer session around a good teacher demonstration, or the challenging but satisfying pupil practical.

The training needs of your teaching staff and technicians will undoubtedly have been identified as a result of your initiatives. Staff development is one of your major managerial responsibilities. Staff development goals may arise incidentally or as a result of formal appraisal, which is another of your responsibilities, within the framework of the school's scheme.

A Head's primary legal responsibility is for the health, safety and welfare of his pupils and of his staff (and for others, such as parents, visitors and workmen who may come on site). You must support him in that general responsibility and you have certain responsibilities in this area vested in you as Head of Science. Make sure you have not inherited, as I did three times, a literally potentially explosive situation! A survey of the whole department – laboratories, preparation rooms, storerooms and, particularly, chemical stores, can be most revealing. Do this in the company of the appropriate colleagues – head of subject and technician, and possibly all the subject staff. This procedure gives early emphasis to your managerial role and to the essential principle in a science department or faculty of division of labour. You may need to do this survey in stages, but do it early and preferably before term begins. If you have been promoted internally, you will already be familiar with the scene, but remember that familiarity breeds acceptance if not contempt. *You* are responsible now and the exercise can help you to confirm the perception in your colleagues' minds of your role and of the responsibilities that they already have.

As outcomes from the survey and from the inevitable and desirable associated consultations, you should be able to confirm to your Head that the following are in place or very soon will be (and will then be confirmed):

a departmental health and safety policy and implementation document (which will relate to and refer to the school's policy document);

sections in that document which detail subject-specific procedures, to include;

micro-biological safety

safety in the storage and use of chemical reagents

safety in the storage and use of radioactive sources

electrical safety (including electrical testing);

you have a registered radiological safety officer (normally the head of physics) and your radioactive sources are stored and used according to current regulations

all chemicals are stored and used according to current regulations. You should note some considerations born of inspecting experience

schools still store reagents which are never used

schools still store reagents they should not hold at all

schools over-stock dangerous and hazardous chemicals which deteriorate over time (including sodium, potassium and white phosphorus)

many chemical stores are too crowded, without proper separation and with incorrect or incomplete labelling

storage in laboratories must take account of both the hazards of the chemicals and the age and stage of pupils who may have access (even if occasionally)

safety carriers should be used between laboratories and storerooms

a colour-coded and position-coded label system helps ensure that reagents get back to the right place;

you have an effective policy over access by pupils to laboratories and preparation rooms. You will try to ensure that laboratories are not used as form rooms but, if they must be, that they are restricted to Sixth Forms;

you have a first aid box in every laboratory and preparation room, appropriately equipped for science teaching environments (for example, with eye-washes) and all staff know how to use them. An ideal aim is for all science teachers and technicians to hold a current first aid qualification – an in-house course arranged directly or through the school's INSET officer is probably the most efficient approach;

identification of any physical hazards which need putting right in the shorter or longer term. (These may be matters for scheduling in your departmental budget or they may be items for discussion with the Head or the bursar for inclusion in the school's capital programme).

Health and safety in the science department is such an important and pervasive matter that you should accept the responsibility but not try to discharge all the detail of the implementation yourself. That is for the heads of subjects, of which you may be one; if so, this would be a useful item of delegation to a subject colleague (although you still have to carry the can!). They will have advice from the subject professional bodies but remember that the ASE is a source of information and advice to all science departments. For that and for other matters, you should be a member of the ASE while you are running a science department.

So far, we have largely considered the Head of Department *within* his department. As far as the Head is concerned a safe, well-run department that is developing new methods for curriculum delivery will engender appreciation and warmth. But even such achievements by the newish Head of Science represent only part of the necessary role from the Head's perspective. The Head must meet him as representative of the Science Department and of science education in the school. You must adopt the role of representative and not that of delegate if you are to be respected by the Head, the deputies and your peers, the other heads of department. What does this mean in practice? That you will be determined to represent your department's views and needs strongly is what your Head will expect. He appointed you because he believed you had the potential to organise your department and guide its development.

But the Head also needs your good counsel, especially since you represent one of the largest and most important curriculum areas. This role demands that you try to share with the Head and his deputies something of their required breadth of vision and their sensitivity to the practicalities of constraints. If you push your department's cause in a blinkered or aggressive way, too greedy for curricular time, too demanding of financial resources, then inevitably there will be two consequences for you. First, the Head, the deputies (and the bursar) will become resistant to your demands so that your reasonable requests are less likely to be successful. Secondly, the Head, his senior colleagues and, very importantly, your fellow heads of department, will lose respect for you as a professional and for your opinions. The ability to recognise that schools are complex places, and that other able colleagues may be competing for resources, are essential qualities in the good Head of Department; as is the quality to recognise that compromises are often a necessity.

If those are the qualities the Head will look for in you, what then are the reciprocals – the qualities that you as a HoD should be able to find in the Head? Some of those I suggest would be reasonable, from experience on both sides of the study door, are the preparedness to listen when you have something you wish to explain; the confidence in you (which you will have to confirm) to leave you to manage your department on a day-to-day basis; and the courage to back you when you want to try some innovative curriculum development. Finally, remember that the more convinced the Head is of the quality of the work you and your department is doing, the more supportive he is likely to be. Much of a Head's work is about planning; so although he could and should take initiatives to visit departments, he will appreciate the specific invitation from time to time – perhaps the testing of the bridge structures from the second form physics course, the display of the first formers' energy folders, viewing the Sixth Form student's micro-video dissection or watching a third form class tackle an interactive assessment via the intranet.

All these initiatives will have developed you as Head of Science and you will doubtless have received generous informal approval from your staff and your envious peers; so, a tactful reminder to the Head about your formal appraisal may be called for. Also, put all your documentation together in a nicely presented departmental handbook ready for inspection!

Chapter 5

Coming ready or not:
ICT across the curriculum

Christopher Jamison
Headmaster, Worth School

Information and communication technology (ICT) is like the person who shouts at the start of a game of hide and seek: "Coming, ready or not!" As Bill Gates wrote in *The Road Ahead* [1] "technology isn't going to wait until we are ready for it." We are none of us ready for what is coming, no more than the monks who copied manuscripts were ready for Gutenberg. Yet the ICT revolution is now far enough advanced for us to have some clues as to what is in store and some hints as to how we might prepare.

The addition of the C to IT to make ICT symbolises the arrival of a second revolution building on the first IT revolution. The processing of information is now established and has reached a plateau; the new revolution is the communications revolution by which the processed information can now be communicated in digital form at high speed to any computer. Thus I not only word process this article (IT) but I can communicate it in an instant whenever I like via e-mail (ICT). So I can communicate this when I like and the receiver reads it whenever they like. This asynchronous nature of digital communication is a key feature opening new horizons: digitised editions of the world's art galleries which I can visit whenever I like, on-line news reports, my own notes available from anywhere in the world whenever I want to access them and so on.

The electronic means of communication are converging, with telephony, television and computers all joining the same digital networks to produce a new communications culture. The extent of this digital revolution is not yet clear but schools have to start meeting it now. Readiness for ICT is the key to making the most of the opportunities now arising. Readiness here involves several aspects of school life and this article will examine those that are of special concern to Heads of Departments.

There are two levels of ICT readiness: the technical and the psychological. Which comes first? They are, of course, chicken and egg, but if asked to choose one as primary I would choose the psychological level.

Our psychology of education needs to develop to meet the new situation. Put simply, our models of learning in this century have so far been based mainly on Piaget's understanding of how each child's individual cognitive skill develops as he or she grows older. We design courses by asking: how much of the subject can the individual child's brain cope with and retain at this age? With ICT, that basic question is transformed into: how can this class access the subject material available and then present it in manageable form? The second question includes the former question but must now replace it. The shift here is from the student as cultured individual to the student as researching team member.

The implications of this are that the school must be a learning community led by a group of life-long learners called teachers. This, of course, is the classic model of an Oxbridge college – fellows who research and lead the reading of the undergraduates. Secondary schools have not been allowed to use this model; they have been relegated to the level of cramming, never more so than since the invention of the league tables, where quality is measured by exam results. Universities required a toll gate through which only those with high grade exam results could pass and so the learning process was subsumed into the exam process. As teachers, we have bemoaned the exam results culture and I believe ICT gives us permission to escape from this bind. We now have the chance to make all our schools into learning communities on classic Oxbridge lines. The view that secondary education is where you are taught the basics of a subject before becoming an autonomous learner in higher education can now be abandoned.[2] ICT makes available to anybody more even than the world's greatest universities could make available to their scholars; the task of Heads of Department is to be the leaders of this emerging community of learners in our schools.

By now, you may be wondering where are the basics taught within this model and what are the practicalities that enable ICT to make schools learning communities? The answer to both these questions is enormous but a few examples will suffice here.

The basic academic skills are taught very effectively using ICT. For example, Integrated Learning Systems (ILS) such as RM's *Success Maker* are enabling weak maths students to progress 20% faster than their peers with similar IQs. These systems enable the student's exercises to be corrected on the spot by the machine which is programmed to reinforce the topic covered in class, leaving the teacher free to introduce the next topic more quickly. Similarly, the dyslexic student works much more confidently using a word processor and can access information much more readily using an electronic version of reference books on CD-ROM or Internet. Indeed, once any of us has used electronic encyclopaedias, we will usually prefer them for speed and greater flexibility. If you are concerned about basic

Father Christopher Jamison OSB was born in Australia and educated at Downside and Oxford and London universities. He has taught at Worth since 1979 becoming Housemaster, Head of Religious Education and eventually Headmaster in 1994. He was co-author of To Live is To Change *and* Leading IT, *the report of the HMC/GSA IT Working Party, which he chaired. He is a member of the Academic Policy Sub-Committee.*

skills and raising standards, then ICT is for you. Your students will achieve more but with greater autonomy. ICT does not replace current methods but it does offer a greater range of methods. As teachers, our armoury of techniques is broadened and we have more choice in how we shall help pupils make progress. Both whole class teaching and individual needs teaching are enhanced by ICT.

This autonomy is most evident in research for coursework. Your students will now find data of which you are unaware and have not read, whether the topic is a Shakespeare play or the latest results of the Discoverer space probe on Mars. My favourite surprise was to invite my Lower Sixth theology students to write a page of background notes on third century neoplatonism and to be presented next day by a very ordinary Sixth Former with a superb introduction to it written by somebody at Durham University, which he had discovered using the *Yahoo* search engine on the Internet. In fact, the more obscure the topic the more likely you are to gain rapid access to gems such as this; the Shakespeare entries are just too numerous and variable in quality. Your task as a teacher is to enable your students to ask the right questions – the right questions at the start of the research and the right questions once the material is assembled. This is especially necessary with the Internet, which is currently an anarchic mess. The challenge here is for us to teach students how to transform information into knowledge.

The National Grid for Learning (NGL) is the Government's attempt to bring some educational order to this chaos and to co-ordinate school ICT nationally. This initiative will create a way into ICT specially designed for schools involving the following elements: low cost access to the Internet for all school ICT networks; the creation of new on-line materials for schools in partnership with industry; ICT training for all teachers; ICT literacy for all school students. The Independent Schools' Council is currently exploring how independent schools might participate in the NGL. While there will be no govenment funding for hardware/software in independent schools, there may be ways of participating in the government-funded teacher training. Independent schools will also want to be involved in providing high quality learning material through the NGL. HMC, through ISC, will try to keep Heads informed of the progress of discussions about the NGL with the DfEE.

Like the NC, the NGL is going to be a fact of life that independent schools will need to adapt to their own situation; we ignore it at our peril and we will need support from many quarters in order to cope. Yet the most vital task is one that must be promoted from within a school by the HoD, namely staff development. This brings together the psychological and the technical.

Staff development in ICT requires a commitment to several features at once. First, each teacher needs to acquire two kinds of ICT skills: some of the generic skills first (word processing, data bases, Internet use, spread sheets) and then the subject specific skills (modelling in science, design in DT, graphic calculators in maths). I believe that each teacher should have an annual ICT skills development target, either as part of appraisal or as a free standing target.

Secondly, each department needs to undertake the development of teaching techniques to match the new technology, with ICT use clearly specified in teachers' work sheets. In this regard, a recent publication provides invaluable examples of what can be done: *Improve Your Use of IT in Teaching* by Don Passey *et al* [3] is a very practical answer to the plea: what computer based work can the kids do on Monday morning?

Thirdly, departments will examine the shifting psychology outlined earlier, to enable a whole class to work together using new techniques. The teacher will notice a power shift in the classroom; the teaching task has always been to empower others to teach themselves; ICT makes this a more regular occurrence as the student has direct access to a learning resource which does not presume a teacher. For example, whereas a text book usually presumes a teacher, a computer-based package usually does not. The student acquires a greater personal responsibility for learning while at the same time will refer more to other students for help, either in his or her own school or via e-mail. Indeed, plagiarism in coursework via the Internet is now probably impossible to trace and may force us to change our approach to assessment. Our students are increasingly becoming part of a global community of learners and we are running hard to keep up with them.

These three goals require a commitment of resources, especially human resources, and I believe that each school requires an ICT co-ordinator to concentrate on staff needs. The co-ordinator will need to train teachers and will ensure that students are being taught the basic generic skills at agreed times so that teachers know what ICT skills they can expect from their students at any given time. There are different ways of achieving this and these are outlined in Chapter 5 of the HMC/GSA report *Leading IT* [4].

To build on this requires rigorous planning by HoDs to ensure that valuable resources are not wasted. Indeed, if government funding for training becomes available, the HoD will need to draw up a departmental ICT development plan.

Drawing up such a plan would be a good developmental activity for the HoD. It would need to include: an audit of current ICT use; targets for ICT use by pupils in this subject over the next two or three years; the ICT training needed to enable teachers to achieve these targets; use of ICT to deliver ICT professional development; ICT use in school administration. Clearly, much of this will need to be approached by HoDs working together. This will in turn lead to a greater awareness that we are teaching pupils as well as subjects and that departmental walls need to come down to allow progress in this as in other areas of school development.

ICT is not a panacea for all our educational needs. It is, however, more than a giant gimmick and more than a gigantic machine for doing tedious tasks quickly. ICT is now emerging as a culture shifting force, especially in our educational culture. *Leading IT* offers Heads insights into how to establish the framework of ICT in their schools and HoDs might benefit from reading that report themselves. This article complements that report and suggests how HoDs can carry this task forward. The final paragraph of the report will also make a fitting conclusion here:

> Our schools will be operating within this information society and will want students to acquire the skills which match the priorities of that society. More than any other sector of education, independent education must be responsive to parental demands. We believe that these demands will change rapidly as the information society establishes itself, causing schools to reassess their approach to learning. Whatever the political and social demands on education at present, future demands will be for schools to initiate students into life-long learning in the information society. [5]

1 The Road Ahead *(1995) by Bill Gates (Viking Penguin).*

2 *This has already happened with GNVQs which have a very different learning style to A levels.*

3 *Folens Publishers, Albert House, Apex Business Centre, Boscombe Road, Dunstable LU5 4RL.*

4 Leading IT *pp 27-30. Available form HMC, 130 Regent Road, Leicester LEI 7PG for £5.*

5 *ibid. pp37.*

Chapter 6

Mathematics or numeracy?

Stuart Westley
The Master, Haileybury

The epidemic of change which has struck British education in recent years has left no part of the system untouched and the teaching of Mathematics has been no exception. While teachers have struggled to adjust to the changing requirements of the National Curriculum, modified A levels, the advent of modular A levels to mention a few, there has been little fundamental analysis of the differing needs of pupils. The temptation to advocate a period for consolidation of recent changes and one of relative tranquillity is compelling. Unfortunately there is disturbing evidence concerning the way in which the subject is now taught in schools which suggests that further fundamental revision is unavoidable as soon as the current moratorium on change is over, including asking whether a single prescriptive curriculum to age 16 is appropriate at all.

The London Mathernatical Society, the Engineering Council, The Institute of Mathematics and its Applications have all recently reported in detail on the inadequate understanding of Mathematics which they observe in their students on a daily basis. These are influential bodies whose members are in a position to know and whose judgments, even those of an intuitive nature, are not easily discredited. The deficiency not surprisingly is said to lie in the higher order skills associated with algebraic analysis, understanding of the importance of precision and proof, the ability to solve complex problems which are not broken into discrete steps as is now the fashion in school examinations and the facility to handle number without recourse to a calculator or computer. The reports' clearly documented evidence strongly suggests that the level of understanding of mathematical principles among current undergraduates studying Mathematics and applied sciences has reduced very significantly in the last decade.

The other conspicuous symptom that all is far from well lies in the rapidly declining take up of Mathematics as an A level subject. In response to a massive concern among those involved in teaching Mathematics the matter was investigated by the Schools Curriculum and Assessment Authority who subsequently reported their findings in June 1996. In the first paragraph of its analysis of recent trends the Report concludes that the number of A level candidates taking Mathematics and Science has remained broadly constant over the past few years but the proportion specialising in Mathematics and Science (that is those taking only Mathematics or Science A levels) has declined. Substantially more of the students who take Science and Mathematics A levels now do so in combination with one or more humanities subjects.

No cause for urgent concern there one might reasonably suppose! That conclusion however significantly makes no reference to the greatly increased staying on rate, post-16, and the corresponding increase in A level subject entries. When assessed against overall A level entries a very different picture emerges, clearly documented within the Dearing Report which acknowledges that the proportion of A level students specialising in Mathematics and the Sciences has declined in recent years from 30% in 1984 to 17% in 1995. The migration from Further Mathematics is equally if not even more disturbing; the number entering for that examination fell from 5600 in 1990 to 4100 in 1995, a decline of almost 27% in five years!

After school at Lancaster Royal Grammar School, Stuart Westley read law at Corpus Christi College, Oxford. A brief and unspectacular spell in first class cricket was accompanied by teaching during the winter at King Edward VII School at Lytham, Lancashire. Subsequently he was Housemaster and Director of Studies at Framlingham College, Suffolk (1973-1984); Deputy Headmaster of Bristol Cathedral School (1984-1989); Principal, King William's College, Isle of Man (1989-1996) and is currently Master of Haileybury.

The SCAA Report attempted to analyse take up for Mathematics and Science A levels against school characteristics. It found that A levels in Mathematics, Physics and Chemistry were most popular in independent and grammar schools, least popular in comprehensive and secondary modern schools. The well known gender pattern was confirmed with take up for those three subjects being strongest in boys' schools. While the advent of modular A levels was frequently put forward as a factor which significantly increased popularity, the Report surprisingly found little evidence that this was actually the case. The purpose of the Report was to analyse rather than explain and, taken together, the outcomes shed very little light on the cause for the diminishing take up of Mathematics and physical science at A level.

That the decline was clearly underplayed if not understated is a matter of concern in itself. Recent work on comparability studies between A levels strongly suggests that Mathematics is one of the subjects in which it is more difficult to achieve the higher grades by a factor of approximately half an A level grade. Though the axioms on which those conclusions are based might appear open to question the research itself has won widespread respect on account of its extensiveness and thoroughness. The problem facing those concerned with the teaching of Mathematics was neatly summarised in paragraph 10.72 of the Dearing Report that in relation to GCSE the requirement of Mathematics A level is more demanding than that of other subjects while simultaneously the adequacy of A levels as a preparation for university is seriously in doubt.

Whatever commendation the Dearing Report might attract on account of its directness and honesty in describing the problems currently associated with the teaching of Mathematics, there can be far less enthusiasm for the proposed responses. Concerning the gap between the GCSE and A level neither of the two recommendations of the Report conveys much credence. The first is to encourage schools and colleges whose students propose to take A level also to take the GCSE in Additional Mathematics together with a recommendation to the examination authorities to enable it. This traditional route is well known and inevitably presupposes early entry for GCSE Mathematics. It is difficult to believe that many schools which have the resources and the will to introduce Additional Mathematics and the consequent early GCSE entries are not already doing so.

This is little more than a reminder about an existing opportunity. It should be noted that early entries inevitably imply acceleration from an earlier stage of secondary education, in other words a form of differentiation and that may contain the seeds of a more radical and more effective reform. Additional Mathematics has many admirers as a preparation for A level; it is demanding both conceptually and regarding the extent of its syllabus. What is to be its relation to the new horizontal AS in Mathematics? This is a question Dearing poses and leaves to others to answer, and presumably to consider whether Additional Mathematics has a place at all if the new AS establishes itself in a way which its predessors manifestly did not. The second recommendation proposes additional resource material to provide courses to bridge the gap between GCSE and A level which is laudable in itself but unlikely to make more than minimal inroads into the problems.

Subsequent recommendations are even more unconvincing. In response to the concerns expressed in the consultation phase, presumably from those working in Higher Education, the recommendation is that the appropriate SCAA Committee consults with the awarding bodies to reappraise the size of the mandatory core within all A level syllabuses, a road which has been travelled before. The next recommendation, that schools and colleges should encourage students to make more use of Further Mathematics, will be ill-received in those schools which have neither students able to cope with that demanding subject nor staff available to teach them. There are further tentative recommendations to consider the introduction of A level syllabuses which are either limited by content or limited by level. Both ideas seem fundamentally flawed. Limitation by content appears to derive from the desire to provide only that part of the A level syllabus which might be relevant to students' subsequent needs at university, assuming, very dubiously, that they are ascertainable at the outset of the Sixth Form career. Limitation by level, that is allowing access to only a limited range of A level grades, causes one to question the likely popularity of such syllabuses, not to mention their comparability with standard A level and GNVQ. Both concepts are at odds with the principle of reduction in number and simplification of A level syllabuses.

The post-Dearing phase has involved an extended period of consultation over the provision for those in education beyond the end of compulsory schooling which is not yet complete. There is however a widespread assumption that the Dearing recommendations are by no means the final word. Among the many matters currently open to consultation are two which are likely to have a considerable impact on the teaching of Mathematics in our schools. Fundamental to the current debate is the question of breadth and its possible delivery by means of an overarching qualification which would require students to achieve success, however defined, in several different areas of the curriculum. The matter has been on the agenda for at least a decade with the Higginson Report of the late 1980s and its summary dismissal still in the memory of many.

If the government grasps that potentially very painful nettle and ushers into the provision for 16-to 19-year-olds a Baccalaureate style qualification then Mathematics for all pupils in the Sixth Form is a realistic prospect, much to be welcomed. A less prescriptive approach in which breadth is encouraged without being required will also substantially increase the number of pupils studying Mathematics after age 16. The other area of uncertainty is the future status of Key Skills and, in the Mathematics context, the future of 'The Application of Number'. Dearing envisaged assessment by a new 'AS in Key Skills' (Recommendation 64) which the majority of students would be encouraged to take though it would not be a requirement for the award of A level. This proposal too leaves many important and basic questions unanswered including whether the examination is intended for the specialist mathematician and the non mathematician simultaneously, hardly a realistic prospect!

Heads of Mathematics and Directors of Studies will have a shared anxiety over the future teaching provision which they must offer and somehow fit into the other timetable constraints. While the way forward remains unclear many will opt for the tried and tested route of three A levels, confident that it is workable and the currency which Higher Education knows and understands. Many will already be committed to early entries and fast-tracking for all pupils who can benefit, leading to earlier examination entries at both GCSE and of the increasingly popular A level modules. The ambitious may have taken advantage of independence to make explicit exactly how their schemes of work extend beyond the confines of the National Curriculum, introducing an enhanced content of scholarly Mathematics into what, in the Key Stage Three years at least, is largely numeracy.

The level of mathematical attainment of entrants to our schools will also be of concern and there will be at least a cautious welcome for the 'Back to Basics' campaign of the present Government. While we may wonder how we have managed to regress so far from respected and tested methods the overall tenor of the preliminary report of the Numeracy Task Force, January 1998, addressing the teaching of Mathematics in the primary years, is much to be welcomed. The recommendations are thorough and full of sound sense; they address the training of teachers, including their continuing training, in addition to teaching methods. The report should be of interest to Heads of Mathematics in senior schools and is perhaps a herald of an era when achievement really is to triumph over ideology.

The current situation reveals well documented problems of near crisis proportions and after a decade of ceaseless change and inquiry only a few somewhat superficial ideas in the published material as to how to address them.

A radical approach would involve an entire rethink of the philosophy behind National Curriculum Mathematics. A central and fundamental assumption is that one programme of study is suitable for pupils of all abilities. That assumption should be challenged and particularly scrutinised in its application to younger pupils in the primary and preparatory schools. To assume that some at least of the higher order mathematical skills, including sequential reasoning, abstraction and proof, cannot be communicated to some pupils of quite young age is a dangerous and all too common fallacy. There is little doubt that through its clarity and detail the National Curriculum has made the acquisition of numerical skills much more accessible for many school pupils who would never find satisfaction or benefit in study of abstract Mathematics. For them the advent of attainable targets and the opportunity to acquire confidence and fluency in their understanding of number and other relevant and accessible concepts is an unqualified blessing. This dimension has been described as primarily social but its benefit should not be underestimated on that account.

Despite the beguiling phrases called in aid to trumpet current policy, 'preparing pupils for adult life', 'learning how to learn' and all the rest, much of National Curriculum Mathematics is devoid of anything genuinely intellectual and therefore is a disservice to the mathematically able and ambitious. Many pupils who from a very early age could catch a glimpse of the true nature of this most exacting and satisfying of disciplines are denied it through the rigidity of the curriculum forced upon them and the dearth of teachers capable of communicating the simplicity, universality and beauty of the subject.

It is not just those who will proceed to university to study Mathematics or the many Mathematics- related subjects who stand to benefit but all who have the capacity to develop the ability to think conceptually and who wish to contemplate beyond the immediately measurable. The challenge is to proclaim the need for differentiated provision for pupils from an early age in the primary stage and for those with mathematical understanding to raise their voices and make themselves heard. Part of pupils' entitlement is that those who can comprehend the truth and beauty of abstract Mathematics should be offered at least a glimpse of it. The statutory documents as presently constituted communicate very little recognition of Mathematics as a source of truth, rigour and beauty. This is a shortcoming which mathematicians in independent schools have the opportunity to recognise and, by virtue of their independence, to address. Only their own pupils could benefit of course, but that is another story!

Chapter 7

Enter the world of Quangoland: The role of the national education agencies

Philip Evans
Head Master, Bedford School

It does not sound an exciting title, and indeed I must be careful not to fall into the trap of providing a sterile bullet point list of the function of national education agencies. I shall try to make what follows palatable and, in sympathy with many government organisations these days that seek to gain the 'Crystal Mark' for clear English, as free from jargon as possible.

Jargon *is* an issue. Having served as a government adviser since 1991, I know how easy it is to move into Quango-speak, a form of communication that appears perfectly reasonable to those who have rubbed shoulders in Quangoland, but which sounds bizarre and other-worldly to the ordinary mortal.

I well remember when I was a classroom teacher that my then association, AMMA, produced what they termed a 'Jargon Generator' which consisted of nothing more than three columns with a list of words or phrases in each column. By linking any phrase in column one with another in column two and a third in column three, one could produce the most extraordinary terms such as 'criterion referenced cognitive reinforcement' or 'conceptualised iterative assessment', which sounded full of authority but which were in fact meaningless. As if to prove my point, I did try on occasion dropping such phrases into conversation in the many committees on which I sat, to find no reaction from my fellow committee members other than silent head-nodding as it was recognised that one of the speakers had gone into committee mode.

It is important that I do not move into such a mode when writing about national education agencies. These agencies *are* important, and their deliberations are often far reaching in terms of what is done in the classroom, what is assessed and what is reported. It is also fair to say that the Civil Servants servicing the many committees of these organisations are highly able, hard working and intelligent people, whose loyalty to the organisation is only equalled by their own commitment to ensuring the success of government education policy. It is all too easy to scoff at what such agencies do, or the motives which lie behind their deliberations but in my experience, while mistakes are indeed made at times, they are at least made in genuine error and with the best of motives. When we think of our own schools and some of the initiatives we have introduced, it is easy to see that mistakes can be made even when research has been extensive and the people driving the changes highly competent. I do not share the cynicism – I would say that, wouldn't I – with which some people view our national agencies.

So let us consider our first 'agency', the jewel in the crown, which is of course the **Department for Education and Employment** (DfEE). This was established in July 1995 with the merger of the former Department for Education and most of the former Employment Department, though some activities here

Dr Philip Evans is Head Master of Bedford School and was previously Head of Chemistry at St Paul's. He has been a Government adviser since 1991, and is presently a member of the Qualifications and Curriculum Authority. A scientist by training, he has served various education committees of the Royal Society and the Royal Society of Chemistry. He attends the HMC Academic Policy Sub-Committee.

were moved to other Departments. With employment now linked to education it represents – and it is particularly true with this Government – a linking of education with the world of work which is consistent with a commitment to life-long learning.The earlier DfE emerged from the Department of Education and Science, you'll recall. It would be an interesting debate to discuss what emphases and changes have led to the DES ultimately becoming the DfEE.

The role of the DfEE is to support economic growth and to improve the nation's competitiveness and quality of life by raising standards of educational achievement. Its role also includes raising standards of skills. This is again consistent with the change over recent decades to see education, not simply in terms of what is known or what is remembered, but also by what can be *done*. One of the crucial ways in which the DfEE sees this economic growth and increased competition occurring is by promoting an efficient and flexible labour market. From this Government's point of view the link between education and employment is a most crucial one, and much will be understood of the Department's thrust in the next few years if this point is kept in mind.

The Department has many responsibilities of course. It seeks to ensure that children, young people and adults achieve skills and qualifications to the highest standard of which they are capable. It is also required to monitor how quickly we are progressing towards the National Targets for Education and Training. These targets are hugely ambitious, and it is not clear to me how they might be achieved. For example, to achieve the target set for the turn of the century in terms of the proportion of the cohort gaining five grades A* to C at GCSE demands a further increase in the slope of the present graph of achievement against time, a graph which has already been criticised because of the grade inflation it is seen to represent. Additionally, while the Department recognises the need to equip young people for the responsibility of adult life in the world of work, it also aims to encourage lifetime learning so that skills can change as appropriate to allow adults to cope effectively with changes in the labour market.

The Department is also working towards the development of what it describes as a 'coherent framework' of high quality national qualifications for all ages which will reflect both academic and vocational achievement. As far as independent education is concerned, the major issues here are the development of the 14 to 19 continuous curriculum and the post-16 issue, which are occupying a large number of able minds at the time of writing. The Department also sees the promotion of the advancement of understanding and knowledge across all subjects as important, and seeks to underpin this support by itself supporting high quality research. Because of its employment focus, it also aims to provide a framework by which employers are encouraged to invest in the various skills needed for competitive business, as well as going beyond that and seeking to help unemployed people into work. If we add equal opportunity issues in education at training and at work (particularly with regard to gender, race, disability, and 'ageism'), we can see how powerful and broad ranging is the Department's remit. All this of course has now to be placed in a new and broader context as well, given the importance this Government attaches to building strong links within the European Community.

The next place to stop is perhaps the **Office for Standards in Education** (OFSTED). OFSTED is a non-ministerial government department and is headed by her Majesty's Chief Inspector of Schools (HMCI) who is at the moment Chris Woodhead. A good deal of humorous material has been written about OFSTED, most notably perhaps by Ted Wragg in his *TES* column, but I shall restrain myself from seeking to add to this. OFSTED was set up in September 1992 under the Education Act to keep the Secretary of State for Education and Employment informed about issues concerned with education standards. The major strands of the remit are monitoring the quality of education in schools in England (separate inspectorates exist for Wales, Scotland and Northern Ireland); the educational standards that are achieved in those schools; whether the financial resources made available are managed efficiently; and the moral, spiritual, social and cultural development of peoples at those schools.

It is also worth noting that although OFSTED was established in 1992, Her Majesty's Inspectorate has existed since the late 19th century. Indeed there was much criticism that Kenneth Clarke, the then Secretary of State, in establishing OFSTED was essentially further privatising the Inspectorate and reducing its independence as well. Subsequent events, particularly with Chris Woodhead's trenchant view of his role, have shown that such concerns were largely unjustified. Some might disagree here, seeing a certain degree of politicisation, but overall it is fair to say that OFSTED has largely maintained its independence from government.

The central remit of OFSTED, then, is to improve standards of achievement and quality of education through regular independent inspection, public reporting and informed advice. This advice is often made within the many publications that OFSTED produces during the course of the year. Such publications are more approachable and even hard-hitting than they once were; many are well worth reading.

In clarifying the role of OFSTED, it is important to make a distinction between the work of HMI and that of the registered inspectors within their teams. HMI are on the staff of OFSTED, but registered inspectors are not; they simply carry out the inspections under contract to OFSTED. There are four categories of independent inspectors: registered inspector, team member, lay inspector and registered nursery inspector.

OFSTED has its headquarters in London, plus a network of 12 regional offices. HMCI is supported by two directors of inspection and 17 teams report to the directorate. OFSTED retains close links not only with the DfEE but also with other government organisations such as the Qualifications and Curriculum Authority, the Higher Education Funding Council, the Further Education Funding Council as well as OFSTED counterparts in Scotland, Wales and Northern Ireland. In addition OFSTED keeps in contact with LEAs, employers and their organisations and other bodies with an interest in education and inspection. OFSTED also has contact with inspectorates in other countries and is an active member of the Standing International Conference of Inspectorates.

Those staff appointed as Her Majesty's Inspectors also inspect schools, teacher training, LEAs and LEA-funded further education – a wide brief. On the basis of these inspections, the Chief Inspector then advises the Secretary of State and the DfEE, as well as other government departments and national bodies, on standards of achievement and the quality of education.

The staff within OFSTED provide management and personnel functions, financial services, run the system of competitive contracts for continuing regular inspection, provide quality assurance for the system, interpret and report on inspection findings and consult other organisations with an interest in OFSTED's work.

So OFSTED responsibilities include the establishment and maintenance of a system for regular inspection by independent inspectors of all state-funded schools in England, as well as offering advice to the Secretary of State on any matter connected with schools or with particular schools. It is also required to promote efficient inspections by encouraging competition between registered inspectors (under the 1996 Act, alternative arrangements for the inspection of a school can be made if it is not practical for it to be inspected by a suitable registered inspector). Even though the independent sector has developed its own systems of inspection, OFSTED retains responsibilities not least for registration visits and for those independent schools outside the ISC.

It also, as indicated above, has a role to inspect and report on the quality of further education in this area. It looks at the standards achieved and the efficient use of resources made available in LEA-maintained or assisted institutions of further education. It is also required to inspect and offer advice to the Teacher Training Agency – more later – as well as the DfEE on all providers of initial teacher training. With the new nursery education provision, OFSTED is required to arrange inspection of such provision (not covered by the School Inspections Act 1996) which includes arranging for the training and registration of nursery inspectors and monitoring inspections for quality. Under the 1997 Education Act, it is also required to inspect any function relating to the provision of education of pupils made by the LEAs and to inspect any function of an LEA when requested by the Secretary of State. Clearly, OFSTED is busy, and has a very broad-ranging remit. Given this remit, and the high public profile taken by the present HMCI, the role of OFSTED in influencing government thinking is undeniable.

The Qualifications and Curriculum Authority (QCA) is perhaps the most relevant proper quango to move to first. QCA was established as a Non-Departmental Public Body by the Education Act of 1997 and brought together, and indeed expanded upon, the functions of both SCAA and NCVQ in promoting the advancement of education and training in England. Under its Chairman, Sir Bill Stubbs, and Chief Executive, Dr Nicholas Tate, QCA has a daunting range of responsibilities. Most obviously, it has to advise the Secretary of State, keep under review and carry out research. On all matters related to the curriculum and school examinations assessment of maintained schools in England. It also publishes and disseminates all information relating to the curriculum, examinations and assessment for maintained schools. Areas of responsibility which are less well-known, perhaps, is that QCA is also tasked to develop learning goals and related materials for children receiving nursery education in England as well as accrediting baseline assessment schemes for children entering primary schools.

It is perhaps in relation to external qualifications (and this includes any externally awarded academic or vocational qualification, other than academic qualifications of first degree level or above) in England and Wales that QCA's work is most rigorous. It must collaborate with the Welsh quango ACCAC (more later) and as far as NVQs are concerned with Northern Ireland, to keep under review all aspects of external qualifications and to advise the Secretary of State, and carry out research, on matters relating to them. It also has to provide support and advice to all bodies which provide courses leading to external qualifications in order to maintain high standards in these qualifications. As well as publishing and disseminating information relating to external qualifications, it also has to develop and publish criteria for these qualifications and to accredit all external qualifications that meet those criteria. These are broad powers and indeed, broad responsibilities. One other important part of QCA's remit, but in relation to England only, is to advise the Secretary of State on exercising his powers under Section 37 of the Education Act 1997, which relates to the approval of external qualifications, and to exercise any functions under that Section at his direction. It is clear from all this that QCA is essentially the 'Curriculum and Assessment Board' for all students aged between five and 18 in this country. In essence, no examination can be accredited without QCA giving an imprimatur.

We can trace the history of QCA from all its predecessor bodies: the Schools Council, the School Examinations and Assessment Council, the National Curriculum Council, the School Curriculum and Assessment Authority, the National Council for Vocational Qualifications; all this has led to QCA, which has now concentrated within it the most extensive remit and the greatest powers of any educational quango seen in this country.

Next stop is the **Qualifications Curriculum and Assessment Authority for Wales**. The acronym (ACCAC) is derived from the Welsh name of the Authority. ACCAC was first established as an NDPB, under the sponsorship of the Welsh Office, by the Education Reform Act 1988 as the Curriculum Council for Wales (CCW). Successive Education Acts, first in 1993 when it was renamed the Curriculum Assessment Authority for Wales, and the Education Act 1997, further expanded its role. It now works essentially as the QCA for Wales. Indeed, its role is formally described as being 'to promote quality and coherence in education and training in Wales' and when one looks at its responsibilities, they tie closely to those of QCA in England. This will and has at times already led to difficulties, where a decision made by ACCAC does not agree with a decision made by QCA, producing a mis-match in education provision between England and Wales. Since the educational systems are closely linked, and essentially modelled on the same system, this may in future cause further difficulties. On a day-by-day basis, however, QCA and ACCAC are expected to work coherently and well together.

The **Scottish Qualifications Authority** (SQA) was established in 1996 as an NDPB by the provisions of the Education (Scotland) Act 1996 which merged the functions of the Scottish Vocational Education Council (SCOTVEC) and the Scottish Examination Board (SEB). The role of the SQA is to develop and award most of the qualifications in Scotland's schools, colleges, workplaces and other training and education centres, other than – as for England – higher education centres. SQA is the certificating body for qualifications in the national education and training system in Scotland. It is also the main awarding body in Scotland for work qualifications; it is Scotland's accrediting body for SVQ qualifications, the equivalent of the English NVQs.

The responsibilities of the SQA are therefore clear. It develops and credits awards, and keeps under review all qualifications that were previously available from both SCOTVEC and SEB. It also administers and certificates the new *Higher Still* courses and awards which, from 1998, as many of us in England and Wales will not know, will replace Highers, Certificate of Sixth Year Studies, National Certificates and GSVQs. The Scots have a high regard for their educational system, and it is worth remembering that it has moved on still further following the recommendations of the Howie Report. SQA maintains records of qualification achievements in Scotland and administers the National Record of Achievement there. It also credits SVQs to national standards and criteria, thereby seeking to ensure that there is some mutual recognition with NVQs in England.

Staying in Scotland, I move on to the **Scottish Consultative Council on the Curriculum** (SCCC) which was established in 1988 as another NDPB under the sponsorship of the Scottish Education Industry Department. The role of this quango is to sustain and enhance the curriculum offered in Scottish schools for the benefit of the whole community. It is therefore the equivalent of the now defunct NCC in England. It keeps the curriculum under review and advises the Secretary of State for Scotland on matters requiring attention. In addition to this it carries out programmes of curriculum development and provides guidance to schools, local authorities and others, and ensures the provision of support for such schools and LEAs.

SCCC personnel can offer help and advice to schools in the planning, development and implementation of a national curriculum, in the production and publication of school teaching materials, in staff development for Headteachers and teachers and in the managing of change in schools. As many of us who have sought to discuss matters with QCA and its predecessor body SCAA will know, asking questions of officers of these quangos often leads to good advice being given. Certainly those who have taken the initiative to ring up to ask a question of someone in SCAA, for example, have found them uniformly helpful and knowledgeable.

In Northern Ireland, the QCA role is taken over by the **Northern Ireland Council for the Curriculum, Examinations and Assessment** (CCEA). This Northern Ireland Council is a non-departmental public body and, just like QCA, is a statutory body with both operational and advisory functions. CCEA was established under the Education and Libraries (Northern Ireland) Order 1993 and began its work in April 1994. Its role is to provide advice to the Northern Ireland office on curriculum, assessment and examination matters. It is also responsible to Northern Ireland for the implementation of Key Stage Three testing, administration of all transfer procedures and indeed the conduct of GCSE and GCE examinations. Its responsibilities therefore mimic those of QCA.

Even the government recognises that the teachers who deliver the curriculum and carry out the assessments are crucial and central to the whole process. The recognition of this came in the formation of the **Teacher Training Agency** (TTA) which was established as an NDPB under the Education Act 1994. This works in England, and in Wales at the request of the Secretary of State and in co-operation with the Higher Education Funding Council of Wales.

The TTA took over the work of the 'Teaching as a Career Unit' and its brief is well known. It is to improve the quality of teaching, to raise standards of teacher education and to promote teaching as a profession. The whole purpose of this is to improve the standards of *pupils'* achievement and the quality of their learning. The TTA also acts as a funding agency, administering funds made available to it by the DfEE and other bodies for the purpose of supporting eligible institutions in England which offer teacher training qualifications. HEFC for Wales has an equivalent role there.

The responsibilities of the TTA are therefore wide-ranging. It is expected to contribute in important ways to the raising of the standards of teaching, and to promote teaching as a career. In seeking to do this, it also aims to improve the quality and efficiency of all routes into the teaching profession. One major aspect of its work is to secure a diversity of high quality and cost effective initial teacher training (ITT), and to secure the effective involvement of schools in all forms of ITT. Beyond this, TTA seeks to promote well targeted, effective and co-ordinated continuing professional development as well as promoting high quality teacher education through the investigation and dissemination of the key features of effective classroom and teaching practice. Conscious that the morale of the profession is tied into how effective is its own professional development, TTA sees such work as extremely important.

Reference was made earlier in this chapter to educational and training targets. QCA, through its curriculum development and its overseeing of effective assessment; OFSTED, through its inspection services; and TTA through the professional development of teachers all have a role in ensuring that national targets are met. The **National Advisory Council for Education and Training Targets** (NACETT) deals with this. NACETT is an advisory body, funded by the government, but which operates independently.

The government of the day appoints NACETT's members, of which half are senior people in business, with the others working in education. The heads of a number of national bodies involved in educational training are members ex-officio. NACETT was established in 1993 to monitor progress towards the national targets, to advise government on performance and policies that influence progress towards those targets (which as I said earlier are highly ambitious), to provide business leadership in raising skill levels, and to increase employment commitment to those targets.

NACETT'S basic responsibilities are to raise the percentage of people who achieve two A levelsby the age of 21, have advanced GNVQ or an NVQ level three, as well as raising the percentage of the cohort who by the age of 19 are achieving five GCSEs at grade C or above, or the equivalent via the GNVQ Intermediate or NVQ level two. NACETT is also tasked to raise the percentage of people by age 19 achieving NVQ level two competence in communication, numeracy and IT (the basic skills) as well as raising the percentage of those achieving level three competence in these important core skills by the age of 21.

With Information Technology and the World Wide Web being increasingly important in all our everyday lives, I now move on to describe the role of an important NDPB. **The British Educational Communications and Technology Agency** (BECTA), formerly the National Council for Educational Technology 'is the national focus of expertise for technology and learning'. It is a company limited by guarantee with charitable status. NCET was with us for some time, as it was formed in April 1988 by the amalgamation of the Council of Education Technology (CET) with the Microelectronics Education Support Unit (MESU).

The members of BECTA are appointed by the Secretary of State for Education and Employment, the Secretary for Scotland and the Secretary of State for Northern Ireland. BECTA is therefore funded from the Education Departments of England, Scotland and Northern Ireland as might be expected. Further funds are, however, derived from specific contracts with other bodies. As a non-statutory body, BECTA relies on persuasion, dissemination of evidence and good practice to influence the educational system and its success has depended on its ability to build effective partnerships, particularly with statutory agencies. Its clear role is to influence change within the educational system and to encourage the effective use of technology and learning. Its responsibilities are broad. It seeks to persuade institutional decision makers to implement education technology in an effective fashion by supplying them with sound evidence on the importance and role of technology.

It also seeks to advise and influence government departments, statutory bodies as well as LEAs on the development of coherent policies for education technology. As might be expected, it also seeks to liaise with providers of product services and training to improve the quality, availability and uses of education technology. It also looks at the future, as it monitors new technologies and seeks to maintain an objective overview of innovative practices in order to assess their potential for meeting educational needs.

The **Basic Skills Agency** (formerly the Adult Literacy and Basic Skills Unit) is the national agency for basic skills for England and Wales, funded primarily by the DfEE and the Welsh Office. The Basic Skills Unit was established in 1995, and although it is funded via central government, it is an independent organisation with a board of management including representatives from LEAs, TECs, employers, trade unions, voluntary organisations, FE colleges and other national and training organisations.

Basic skills are defined as 'the ability to read write and speak English and use Mathematics at a level necessary to function and progress at work and in society in general'. In Wales basic skills includes the ability to read and write Welsh for people whose mother tongue it is. Its role is therefore a relatively straightforward one to outline. It is to develop basic skills programmes to adults and to support and develop an effective programme for children and young people. Given that the effectiveness of education at secondary level is based on the competence that children gain at primary level in the basic skills, it is clear how important the work of the Basic Skills Agency actually is. Its responsibility is to prevent failure, particularly early failure. If failure has been identified, its role is then to help children and young children catch up. It also aims to encourage adults to improve their basic skills. It seeks to help to raise standards through the promotion of relevant support mechanisms: publications, staff training, national research, a focus on family literacy and by an enthusiasm to embrace effective new developments.

So there we are – a summary on the role and responsibilities of the various national educational organisations. They do change from time to time, of course. If we track, as I have done above, the history of the Schools' Council through to QCA, the general thrust of these organisations has been, driven by government of course, to increase their remit and their power. Sometimes they are seen as grey bureaucratic organisations; but it is reassuring to remember that they have people within their buildings who are uniformly committed to raising educational standards in the country. You may not always agree with their methods or with what they are seeking, or how they seek to do it, but it is difficult to quarrel with their overarching aims.

Quangoland is important; it is also a little less faceless than one might suppose. If you can, do take the opportunity to become involved: respond to consultations, offer your services if you have expertise in particular areas, perhaps on standing committees, and most of all remember that we are all seeking the same outcome. This is an effective and acceptable entitlement for education in this country, not simply for the five to 18-year-olds but beyond. "Learning is for life", says this Government; it also sees its priority as "education, education, education".

I think these are emphases with which we can all identify.

Chapter 8

Modular A levels

James Miller

Headmaster, Royal Grammar School, Newcastle upon Tyne

According to Roger Porkess (Project Leader of MEI) and the evidence of two surveys that I have carried out into the experience of, respectively, HMC and HMC and GSA schools[1], the first modular A level in independent schools was a pilot Business Studies programme involving Roedean and The Perse; this was then followed by the pilot of MEI Maths carried out under the auspices of Roger Porkess at Monkton Combe in 1989. In 1990, seven further modular programmes were adopted; in 1991, 24; in 1992, 42; in 1993, 38; in 1994, 333; in 1995, 154. By that stage, the vast majority of HMC and GSA schools were involved with modular A level programmes. By the time of writing, two years later, very few schools will have no experience of modular A levels; indeed, it is becoming increasingly difficult to find wholly linear A level syllabuses.

The initial growth was very much in Mathematics and the sciences, followed by Business Studies and Geography. Recently, things have gone much further, particularly with the trend to the same syllabus and papers, which can be assessed either modularly or linearly. By 1997 most A levels, with the exception of Languages, Art, Design, Technology and Music, were (at least in theory) modular. ULEAC figures for 1997 show that 60% of its A level entry was modular and only 40% linear; and of that 40% three fifths were accounted for by Languages, Art, Design, Technology and Music, *ie* only 16% of their entry was in linear entries in other subjects.

In his review of 16-19 education, Sir Ron Dearing was much exercised by modular A levels, and a series of his recommendations was aimed at them. Though Government has yet to implement these recommendations, some changes will undoubtedly take place in the reasonably near future; This area is considered on page 78.

The pros and cons of modular A levels

The many claimed advantages and disadvantages of current modular A level programmes can be summarised as follows[2]:

Claimed strengths for students

Increased motivation and level of work, particularly in Lower Sixth.

Increased motivation may extend to linear subjects.

Spreading of exam load and reduction of anxiety.

Possibility of resits enables student to demonstrate capability.

Increase in confidence.

Early feedback leads to greater realism

- earlier drop-out if unsuited to A level

- more sensible UCAS choices.

Regular assessment and feedback enhance overall performance.

Earlier realisation that A level is very different from GCSE.

Ability to switch to three module AS reduces possibility of weak student ending two year course with nothing.

Reduction in drop-out rate.

Pupil-friendly chunks.

Banking of modules allows course to be prolonged over four years – a great advantage for mature students and those whose studies are interrupted by illness.

Access to new courses (*eg* Science – valuable, for example, to geographers).

Better results on average, particularly for weaker students.

Claimed strengths for schools
All the advantages as above.

More immediate accountability for teachers.

Possible recovery if teaching approach wrong.

Better UCAS advice and predictions.

Easier joint teaching of A and AS.

Possibility of some joint Lower Sixth/Upper Sixth teaching of some modules.

Improved recruitment.

Earlier and continual feedback enables greater parental support - and reduces the terror and shock of August 17 !

Claimed strengths for UEI
Greater proportion of syllabus is examined[3].

Modular programmes can lead to increase in those doing Mathematics and Science.

Modular programmes can be used to encourage

breadth – via easier access to AS or individual modules

depth – via extension modules.

Claimed weaknesses for students

Some subjects do not lend themselves to full A level assessment in the Lower Sixth[4].

Excessive pressure from continual exams.

Continual disruption from modular exams.

More exam time.

Possible overload from too many resits.

James Miller read Classical Mods and PPE at Oxford, before starting his teaching career at Winchester where, at various times, he was Head of Economics and a Housemaster. He became Headmaster at Framlingham in 1989 and of the Newcastle Royal Grammar School in 1994. He has written articles on the modular approach and accelerated science for university. He is a member of the Academic Policy Sub-Committee.

Priority given by students to modular exams over linear work.

Pressure on extra-curricular activities.

Difficulty of fitting in work for resits.

The "I can always resit" sense of complacency.

Possible demoralisation from bad initial results.

Some students may do better on a linear system.

Some students develop relatively late.

A higher level of achievement required for top grades

Claimed weaknesses for schools

More complex administration *exacerbated* by

The wide range of different modular patterns and dates.

Persistent disruption to the normal life of the school *exacerbated* by

Time off allowed by school or simply taken by pupils before modules.

Difficulty of scheduling resit teaching.

Difficulty of deciding on resit policy for modules done in February/March.

Increase in exam costs.

Possible increase in minimum efficient size of Sixth Form.

The suspicious ignorance of university admissions tutors.

A fear of a lack of coherence in a student's understanding of the subject.

A reduction in the variety of examining method (*eg* essays + multiple choice + short answers + data response) and a difficulty in finding different questions for frequently set papers.

Some subjects (particularly Languages, Art, Design, Technology and Music) simply do not lend themselves to a modular approach; some other subjects (*eg* English, History and Economics) can be handled in a modular fashion – but not necessarily to advantage.

In many schools, much work in many arts subjects in the Lower Sixth is not aimed directly at exams but towards giving the foundation for exam work in the Upper Sixth. This approach does not lend itself to a modular programme.

Some evidence

My 1996 survey tried to investigate the truth of some of the claimed pros and cons. Its findings can be summarised as follows[5]:

Results: modular programmes do, in general, lead to better A level results but the increase is not as large as many have suggested[6]. The improvement at both AB and DE levels is slight, perhaps a quarter of a grade or less on average, though there was a more significant effect noted at AB level in Mathematics. Candidates do better when they retake, by perhaps half a grade, though this may at times be at the expense of later modules taken at the time of the resit.

Demands: the improvement in results is **not** consequent on a decrease in the intellectual demands of modular programmes compared with linear ones. In some subjects, there was a feeling that the demands are greater. Any reductions in demands were felt to be very small, with the largest effects being at the DE levels in Mathematics and English – though even these were minor.

Accessibility: the improvement comes from the fact that modular programmes are more student friendly and lead to candidates working very much harder.

Reaction: modular programmes are very popular with students and popular with parents too. They also lead to an increase in the numbers of students doing the subjects concerned, most notably in Mathematics.

Differences between Boards: it is difficult to draw many conclusions about possible overall differences between exam boards, because the figures are not independent of other variables – *eg* market shares vary across subjects. That said, differences between the exam boards were mainly small, though ULEAC and UODLE seemed to produce a smaller improvement in grades and marginally lower scores for accessibility and pupil reaction.

Effect on linear subjects: students may work much harder on their modular subjects though this is partly (but only partly) at the cost of less work on their linear ones.

Effects on extra-curricular activities: the effects here seem marginal.

Staying on rate: only marginal effects, but given the nature of the schools this is not surprising. The fact that 7% do report an effect is not insignificant.

Exam administration: there are clearly **major** difficulties for exams officers (exacerbated by the variety of different timings and systems) and increases in costs[7].

Time off: only a minority of schools gave more time off than the morning before an afternoon paper. A majority of day schools have run into problems with pupils themselves taking time off before modular exams.

Gender differences: the number of schools reporting any differences in the reactions of the sexes to modular programmes was tiny and the effects small.

The Dearing Review

Dearing was concerned about the possibility that modular A level approaches were less demanding than linear ones particularly because of

"The availability of resits;

The absence of the major challenge represented by the traditional linear A level to master and use effectively in a final examination all the skills, knowledge and understanding achieved over the whole programme. Responding to that challenge is a major achievement by a candidate taking two, three or four A levels at the same time, and such achievement is greater than that of candidates following the modular route whose assessment is spread over 18 months or more." (Dearing: Full Report 10.48)

At the time of Dearing there was a remarkable lack of comparative evidence and, though Sir Ron himself was clearly sceptical about the comparability of modular and linear approaches, he did not make any explicit judgement in his report. His conclusions were as follows:

"The traditional linear A level has stood the test of 45 years. A far higher proportion of the cohort of young people is now successfully pursuing this route than was ever dreamt of when A levels were introduced. Modularity has a great deal in its favour, but there are, for want of a better word, enthusiasms in education for one approach or another, and dangers in an 'enthusiasm' becoming the universal practice, before the full consequences have been digested and evaluated. That process of evaluation takes years. I would therefore advise caution about encouraging or permitting a wholesale change to the modular route, for the following reasons.

We are not yet clear about the effect on school and college management and learning of an A level system committed over the whole subject range to almost continuous external examination. It may be burdensome for schools, distracting for candidates, and damage the quality of learning. Particular concerns have been expressed about the different patterns of examination sessions that have emerged for modular examinations in different boards and the increasing complexity of examination schedules.

It is not certain that it will be feasible in closely focused A level courses to produce a series of fresh questions for each module, so as to avoid predictability of questions.

We have not yet developed an adequate and uniform approach to the intentionally demanding requirement to demonstrate a synoptic understanding of the whole coverage of the A level syllabus in modular schemes.

Subjects lend themselves differentially to the modular approach. Some, like modern foreign languages, in which there is a close integration and relevance to each part of all that is learnt, do not seem suitable for assessment at the full A level standard until well into the course. In others, like English and History, the point during the course at which the assessment takes place makes a difference to the quality of the students' response to examination questions. In Mathematics, where modularity has been practised for several years, there appear to be fewer problems, but the development of ability in algebraic manipulation and an underlying development of mathematical thinking must have some bearing on achievement. This raises two issues: differences between subjects, and the feasibility of questions being at the same level of demand in all modules. The second of these relates to the possibility that early modules should receive a lower weighting than modules taken at the end of the course. This is touched on in Section 11 on the reformulated AS.

The traditional final examination is a demanding test and those who do well in it have a substantial achievement to their credit which universities and employers have learnt to respect." (Dearing: 10.59)

"I recommend that:

1)The regulatory bodies should monitor closely the comparability and consistency of standards in modular and traditional linear A levels and publish an annual report on this.

3) In the meantime, both linear and modular A levels should be retained, but:

the final examination in a modular scheme of assessment should count for not less than 30 per cent of the total marks and should include a number of questions, for which at least half the marks (15 per cent of the total marks for the A level) are reserved, that test understanding of the syllabus as a whole. (No changes are recommended for the traditional linear A level in this respect);

there should be a limit on the number of resits of any one module, to be determined by the regulatory bodies after consultation with the awarding bodies;

the regulatory bodies should monitor closely whether it is possible to maintain a stream of fresh questions for modular examinations to avoid easy question-spotting, particularly in early modules;

the joint committee of the NCVQ and SCAA, with the involvement of Wales and Northern Ireland, should consider whether there should be a common timetable for modular examinations, based on two sittings a year, probably in January and June. They should consider this issue in consultation with the awarding bodies, considering at the same time the timing of GNVQ tests." (Dearing: 10.61)

In addition, a direct consequence of his proposals for a horizontal AS was that initial modules would be less demanding (ie at first year A level standard, rather than all modules being in principle of full A level standard).

Developments since Dearing

At the time of writing (January 1998) there is considerable uncertainty about the results of the Labour Government's review of the Conservative Government's review of Dearing. The following seem probable:

A reduction of modular sittings to just two a year, probably January and June. This is to be wholly welcomed.

The imposition of synoptic assessment in all modular A levels, to try to ensure that candidates have an understanding of the whole syllabus and not just the most recent chunk.

The imposition of a minimum proportion of the syllabus to be examined at the final sitting (likely to be 33%).

It is probable that only one resit of each module will be allowed (though presumably there can be nothing to stop a candidate starting the whole process over again).

Initial modules (leading to a horizontal AS) will be set at first year A level standard and not at what is meant to be full A level standard.

All A level subjects will have modular syllabuses available.

Linear and modular syllabuses will have the same content.

In addition, we can identify the following developments:

An increasing proportion of A levels in subjects that have traditionally not been seen as likely modular subjects (*eg* English and Modern Languages) are becoming modular.

Indeed, linear syllabuses in many subjects are a threatened species, and it is probable that many will in practice die.

It is and will be possible to study a subject in a linear fashion but increasingly only by taking all the modules simultaneously. This runs wholly against one of the ways in which modular A levels have been made as demanding as linear ones; greater examining time has meant that a larger proportion of the syllabus has been tested. If linear exams consist merely of doing all the modules simultaneously, then they are undoubtedly more demanding.

Universities may increasingly start using module results in their decision-making process.

If they do this on the basis of AS results – and in an increasingly competitive world for many universities – make their offers unconditional, there is the risk that candididates will, at best, become very complacent and, at worst, leave school.

Modularity is increasingly coming into GCSE.

There is the horrifying possibility of the following programme for teenagers:

Age 14	Summer	KS3 SATs
Age 15	Summer	GCSE modules
Age 15/16	January	GCSE modules
Age 16	Summer	Complete GCSEs
Age 16/ 17	January	AS modules

Age 17	Summer	Complete AS
Age 17 / 18	January	A2[8] modules
Age 18	Summer	Complete A levels.

On top of this, an increasing number of university courses are becoming semester based and modular with exams twice a year.

We are likely to end up with a system of almost unceasing public assessment, the final collapse of the idea that education is valuable in itself and the marginalisation of non-examined courses.

Advice to Heads of Department

Some subjects clearly lend themselves to a modular approach and your candidates are likely to do better as a result. These subjects include Mathematics, the Sciences and Geography.

Some subjects do not lend themselves to a modular approach, and great care should be taken before you jump on the band-wagon. Such subjects include the practical and creative subjects (*eg* Art, Design, Technology and Music) and Languages.

Beware the "I can always retake" ethos. Retakes (at best) get in the way of subsequent modules and it is very difficult to produce teaching for them. It is vital to work on the basis that retakes are the exception rather than the rule.

Individual departments should not have the right to decide to go modular. Such decisions have knock-on effects on the whole school and should be handled on a whole school basis.

Be *very* nice to your exams officer but reckon that you yourself are going to have to do more exams admin than with linear programmes. Keep a careful eye on entry deadlines. Make sure that your candidates are using the right candidate number.[9]

Do not ask for significant time off before module tests for your candidates.

Expect complaints from your colleagues running linear programmes; they will (rightly) feel that their subjects are getting short shrift when your pupils are coming up to module tests. Tell them that their candidates will have more revision time when final A level exams come up.

Make sure that your teacher i/c calendar and Director of Studies are aware when module tests occur. Make sure that there are no rugby tours *etc* at those periods. Remember that most of your colleagues will not automatically allow for exams in (say) late February. Keep housemasters / tutors *etc* informed, and assume that they will forget what they have been told.

Finding exam halls at module times can be difficult.

Particularly with subjects where modules can be combined in different ways (mainly Mathematics), it is vital that a member of the department who really understands the system is available when A level results come out.

Abandon proper internal exams; your pupils already have enough exams.

Do nothing until the Government makes up its mind.

1 *Ray & Miller:* Modular A Levels *(Oct 1994) and Miller:* Modular A Levels - The Experience of Independent Schools *(Oct 1996).*

2 *This is a slightly modified version of a note of mine included in the appendices to the Dearing Report.*

3 *Not the case if a modular approach has the same assessment regime as a linear one; cf page 79.*

4 *This will cease to be a problem of the Dearing horizontal AS (at 'Lower Sixth' standard) comes in.*

5 *The full report is available from me at the RGS.*

6 *It is quite possible that schools where there is already a strong work ethos may derive less benefit than those where the opposite is the case.*

7 *Most (though by no means all) independent schools recharge parents for exam entry fees; the increase in costs is therefore not a direct concern, though it clearly is for parents. Things are different for those who do not recharge and more importantly for maintained schools.*

8 *'Second year' A level modules (ie those at full A level standard) are given the nomenclature 'A2'.*

9 *All modular candidates are meant to have a Unique Candidate Identifier which can be different from their number for linear A levels.*

Chapter 9

A Scottish perspective

John Robertson
Rector, Dollar Academy

Perceived wisdom would have it that the Scottish education system - like everything else in the developed world - has undergone dramatic, constant change during the past decade. Nothing could in fact be further from the truth.

There have been few major developments (Revised Higher and Certificate of Sixth Year Studies in 1989, Standard Grade in 1987) in the systems of assessment which drive the upper senior school curriculum in most Scottish independent schools, but the background has been one of turmoil. There have been surges of activity, but the overall framework has remained secure.

1991 saw the production of the Howie Report, a report that dared to recommend the equivalencing of the vocational and the academic strands in our system – and the land resounded with fury. Howie had identified many of the problems; his proposals for cure were perhaps not radical enough, and the report was not acted on directly.

The extensive package of reforms thus being compiled at present under the heading of *Higher Still* has brought debate (often acrimonious), union complaints (especially on workload) and warehouses full of magnificently packaged manuals of information. 'Consultation' has been the keynote, as submissions, responses, and responses to responses have filled staff workroom shelves. Radical developments in some traditional subject areas – notably English – are in prospect. The new examination system that should be in place by the millennium will undoubtedly have profound effects on the curriculum and on its management.

Throughout Scotland, Heads of Departments about to deliver *Higher Still* have been mobilised, and it would be fair to suggest that their tensions preceding the arrival of 'the new' are unlikely to diminish. Working through the Guidelines and Action Plans will probably be far more straightforward when the phoney war period ends, and real students in real classrooms are waiting to learn.

In my own school – a strong academic school with a wide, flexible curriculum – Heads of Department have reviewed their roles, with an imaginative focus on what the next four years might bring. Below are listed their expectations for the year

John Robertson, Rector of Dollar Academy since 1994, was Deputy there from 1987 after 14 years in Stewart's Melville, Edinburgh, where he had been Assistant Head. As Principal Examiner in Higher English (SEB), he oversaw the transition to Revised Higher, and has been involved in Scottish curriculum development for many years. He is a member of the Academic Policy Sub-Committee.

2002. From the particular perspective here, a general pattern emerges – significantly, one that stresses the need for continuing professional development for these key individuals in any school.

Expected changes to current practice

Accountability Parental expectations will inevitably rise; departmental expectations of the HoD will likewise become more intense, with classroom teachers putting increased pressure on the HoD to achieve targets for the department as a whole; pupil evaluations of their own learning and of the classroom environment will become the norm.

Examination developments By 2002, the *Higher Still* changes will be firmly embedded, but the proposal that core skills should permeate the curriculum will continue to affect many conventional subject expectations. The management of IT will be central.

Health, safety and security External bureaucratic pressures will increasingly impinge on the governing of schools and directly affect departmental heads, particularly in science subjects.

Initial teacher training While previous attempts to introduce mentoring in Scottish schools have foundered, much of the training of new teachers will devolve to schools.

Communality of resources. Adjusted links in the curriculum will probably lead both to the disappearance of some subjects as we know them and to new varieties of empire building. Financial expediency will dictate the pace of technological developments and this will encourage departments to act co-operatively. There will be little to be gained from departments acting as individual, discrete units.

Development needs for Heads of Department

One Head of Department, whose department's results in external examinations are outstanding, wrote, "I exhibit all the worst features of the under-developed Head of Department ... that mild satisfaction (bordering on smugness) with the present muddle, and a tendency to justify the odd moment of success as a master-stroke of management." With that self-deprecating point in mind, the following needs may be identified:

> Professional development. While subject leaders will continue to be expected to work at the cutting edges of their academic areas of study, the HoD will also be expected to fulfil a range of non subject-specific functions. Thus, in-service provision of modules in time management, motivation, adult psychology, IT, technology in the widest sense, assertiveness training and so on will result.

> A resensitising to the needs of pupils will be required – staff-shadowing of pupils for a period of time could well become more frequent.

Template for the Head of Department in 2002

HoD will have a vigorously positive academic outlook – as presenter of department, as supporter of pupils studying the subject – with 'aggressive cajoling' as the central skill in dealing with both pupils and colleagues.

HoD will be enthusiastic for improvement and development. Members of departments will see mere defensive posturing by Heads of Department as being of little value.

HoD will expect the administration web in the school to work more purposefully to enable a greater focus on learning and teaching in the classroom. This should lead to the removal of many trivial administrative tasks to other personnel, to free time for subject development.

HoD will be confident in monitoring performance of members of department.

HoD will have less direct pastoral responsibility.

HoD will recognise the increasing complexity of decision-making, and 'consultation' (despite the scepticism currently surrounding this term) both inside the department and in wider subject groupings will be the norm prior to action.

New structures

There is little doubt that new posts will need to be created. Significantly, the administration of inter-school links (sporting, musical, artistic, debating and so on) amongst independent schools could profitably come under the aegis of a new style of co-ordinator. The developing links between schools and their local communities will lead to changes in administration, where the bursarial functions, the legal dimensions and the control of the school calendar will lead to a change of emphasis.

Similarly, subject development will demand new and varied skills from subject leaders. As an obvious example, the Director of Music might well have to become a sound engineer, an electronics engineer, and a computer programmer. The technophobe will have few avenues of escape.

Afterthoughts

The Heads of Department involved in this internal survey stressed the value of making available more time for thought. A commitment to the body of knowledge in their subjects was clear and, in a number of instances, there was a call for a change of emphasis from *skills* to *employment of knowledge* once again.

When *Higher Still* arrives in Scotland, the multi-level presentations and the group awards will rapidly be assimilated. A Scottish Parliament, with responsibility for education, will be in place by 2002; new truths will inevitably be told.

And Howie's vision of the merging of the academic and the vocational will very probably have been realised without many actually noticing, and certainly without anyone wishing to reopen the debate.

Chapter 10

Whence the next generation of teachers?

Roy de C Chapman

I was very lucky to be offered a teaching post before I graduated. But this was in the Dark Age of 1959 and I had to make a choice between embarking on a PGCE course or being caught up in one of the very last intakes of National Service. Since I was engaged and since, because of an acute shortage of teachers – *plus ça change* – a College of Education in Edinburgh was offering a seven month course beginning in August, my choice was relatively easy. My decision enabled me both to get married and to take up the post the following April.

Day one at the College of Education was not at all encouraging. In consecutive lectures on the first afternoon, we were informed that the best teaching aid of all was primrose yellow chalk on a green blackboard (*sic*) and then that "all this talk of primrose yellow chalk on a green blackboard is complete nonsense". I have often wondered whether the second lecturer understood the muted – it was 1959 – hoots of derision which rose from his very cynical audience.

Thereafter, my memories are of excruciating boredom, alleviated only by comparing notes with a couple of friends about the "er-um" rate of one of the lecturers in Education. After a few lectures, we noticed that his "er-um" rate was very high at the beginning of a lecture, whenever he moved to a new topic and when he was conscious that the end of the session was close and that he would be allowed no leeway by his restive captive audience. As he lectured, he walked up and down the dais behind the sort of long bench normally found in a science laboratory. In order to add an extra dimension to our research, we tried to draw up a correlation between the turning point at each end of the bench and an "er-um". I have long since forgotten the actual rate of "er-ums" per minute, but the number 16 seems to ring a faint bell. I suppose the lecturer was a classic example of the old saw 'those who *can* teach don't and those who *can't* teach teachers'.

The record will show that at the end of the course, I scored A for Education and D for Psychology. The latter may well explain a great deal in my subsequent career, but I never could – and still cannot – comprehend the connection between bouncing a ball against a wall and the learning process, a connection which appeared to be of fundamental importance in the course.

I must except from my criticism the sessions on methodology in Modern Languages and the periods of teaching practice: one week in a primary school and three blocks of three weeks each in secondary schools. It was my great fortune to be allocated for the first of the latter to the school where Sir Roger Young was the vigorous new broom. He was to become a great influence in my career. My second block of teaching practice was in a tough comprehensive, although if my memory serves me right, that particular term had not been coined at that time. The little wizened lady who taught a particularly difficult class of 15-year-olds gave me only one piece of advice: to keep shut the mouth of the large sprawling lout in the front row.

Happily, the latter took me on in the first few minutes on ground which was very shaky for him and enabled me to deliver a put down which delighted the class (and the little wizened teacher) and kept him quiet for the next three

After being educated at Dollar Academy and St Andrew's University (Harkness Scholar), Roy Chapman took his PGCE at Moray House College of Education, Edinburgh. He was Assistant Master at Glenalmond and Marlborough, and then Head of Modern Languages at Marlborough. He became Rector of Glasgow Academy in 1975 and was Headmaster at Malvern College from 1982 - 1996. He has written two audio-lingual A level text books. He was chairman of HMC in 1994 and now coordinates School Centred Initial Teacher Training for HMC.

weeks. For the record, having found it necessary to look up in the vocabulary at the back of the text book the meaning of the French word 'célèbre', he failed to spot that there were two entries – one as an adjective and one as a verb and he made a fool of himself by insisting on the wrong one in the context long after all the other members of the class had realised that he was wrong and had started to titter at his discomfiture. I must have achieved something during this teaching practice because, before I left the school after my three weeks, I was offered a permanent post for the following April. I had quite a few twinges of conscience about turning it down.

Much has of course changed in the field of teacher training since those very distant days and most of the change has been for the better. However, it always was and still is very difficult to strike the right balance between professional training and teaching practice. Both are of course essential, but opinions vary about the admixture and where the course should be delivered. Really good teachers who enjoy their subject and enjoy the daily contact with their pupils are often reluctant to move away into the field of teaching about teaching and HEIs which have become a refuge for other, *ie* less successful teachers, are manifestly not the right place to be inducting the next generation of teachers. Moreover, the 'others' to whom I refer can so frequently be those who believe that *systems* are an alternative to *personality*. There is so much more to education than teaching.

Lest I be misunderstood, this is *not* intended as a polemic against HEIs in general. However, whether one likes it or not, the shortcomings of a handful of HEIs and the imposition of various ideologies have (unfairly) besmirched the reputation of the majority, and this has led to the regular controversy about whether there is any value in a PGCE course at all. One still hears the argument voiced by a minority of Heads that it is better to go straight into teaching and learn "on the job" – a pretty specious parallel being drawn with hairdressers, who are not best pleased with the parallel either. When it comes to appointing, if all other considerations are equal, an applicant with a PGCE (and a good report on his teaching practice) is likely to take preference over an unknown quantity, but how often are *all* other considerations equal, particularly in subjects with a scarcity of teachers?

Although, for a number of years, Westminster College, the South Bank University and the Open University have offered distance learning PGCE courses for teachers already in post, there was until 1993 no alternative to full-time attendance at an HEI. For some, however, especially graduates considering a second career, *eg* coming out of the armed services or those disillusioned after a period in industry or business, the thought of 'going back to college' before embarking on a career in teaching was abhorrent. Since 1993, there has been the alternative option of a place on a Schools Centred Initial Teacher Training course, where the general professional training as well as the teaching practice takes place *in schools*. And from September 1999, there will be a number of SCITT consortia with HMC schools as the 'lead school'.

A consortium may consist of four to ten schools, although not every school in the consortium will necessarily participate every year. This is principally because the demand for specific subjects will vary from year to year and because individual schools may have reasons for wanting to have a year (or two) out. The ideal consortium will consist of between 30 and 40 trainees, but a consortium can be viable with as few as 20. The 'lead school' provides the base for the delivery of the general professional training, although it will not all necessarily take place there. It also provides the library facilities.

Trainees must have teaching experience in at least two schools where their performance will be supervised and monitored by a Subject Mentor. The general professional training is likely to be delivered by practising teachers from the schools in the consortium together with outside lecturers brought in on an *ad hoc* basis as required, perhaps from the local HEI. This aspect of a trainee's work and progress will be supervised and monitored by a Professional Mentor.

The relationship with a local HEI is likely to be of vital importance to the consortium. It may be invited to act as moderator and validator to the course and to bestow a PGCE qualification at the end of the course. In other words, it is entirely possible for HEIs (and universities) and SCITTs to work together in complementary roles without representing a threat to each other. Some trainees will prefer the ambiance of a college campus with a large number of other trainees, while some again will prefer the possibility of involvement, alongside practising teachers in the whole life of a school community, including extra-curricular activities and the pastoral side.

In the HMC model – incidentally the TTA does not lay down any specific model – the SCITT is set up by the Consortium Consultant and in the first instance by the Head of the 'lead school'. However, once membership of the consortium has been agreed, the Head's role can be rapidly passed on to the Consortium Coordinator who is likely to be of Deputy Head/Assistant Head status and in a position to give about 50% of his/her time to running the consortium on a day-to-day basis. The Consultant's role may diminish once the consortium is operational and initial problems have been resolved, but he or she will continue to be the principal troubleshooter and the first line arbiter of standards (with the validating HEI in the ultimate role) both of the trainees and of the teaching. The whole operation is subject to inspection by OFSTED at any time.

Funding for a SCITT consortium is provided centrally by the TTA and locally by each trainee's local education authority. The funding allows for the Consultant's fee and expenses together with the appropriate portion of the Coordinator's salary, administrative and secretarial expenses, provision of library facilities and a capitation sum for each trainee which can be applied on the basis of an agreed formula by the members of the consortium. In other words, *participation in SCITT does not represent a call on the hard pressed finances of member schools.*

For the *trainee*, SCITT offers the possibility of learning the art (or is it science?) of teaching from experienced practitioners in a situation in which practice in the classroom can be related *in situ* rather than in the abstract to such pastoral matters as discipline, bullying, The Children Act and the place of extra-curricular activities in the overall development of a pupil – thereby avoiding the artificial separation between educational theory and practice.

But what has a *school* to gain by participating in SCITT? A great deal of organisation and hard work is likely to be involved and imposed on an already frenetically over-stretched staff. The mere mention of SCITT in a school common room may give rise to groans of anguish, if not of open revolt. In fact, however, participating schools do have a very great deal to gain in professional terms and nothing to lose in financial terms.

First and foremost there is an important role for Heads of Department but also for Directors of Studies, and those in charge of pastoral matters and extra-curricular activities who are challenged to examine the sort of help, guidance and support which they offer to new teachers. It is no longer enough – actually, it never was –– to present the latter with a thick common room handbook, a teaching timetable, lists of books, lists of pupils and lists of resources and then leave nature to take its course. A new recruit, newly qualified teachers no less than trainees, is likely to be apprehensive and lacking in confidence. There may well be a reluctance to ask questions for fear of appearing foolish or inadequate.

Once trust and confidence have been won, however, trainees should be emboldened to exercise their critical faculties and to challenge why things are done in a certain way. From time to time, they may even be able to suggest better ways of doing things. It can be taken for granted that trainees are unlikely to accept the explanation (or justification) "that's the way it's always been". It can also be taken for granted that trainees who have chosen the SCITT route will be eager to participate as much as possible in the corporate life of the school and, wisely used, they can provide an extra pair of eyes and an extra pair of hands in all sorts of areas, outside the classroom no less than in it.

The fact that the general professional training takes place in schools instantly underlines the close link between theory and practice. Lectures and discussions on the theory, philosophy and psychology of education no less than nuts and bolts topics such as The Children Act, bullying, learning difficulties, the responsibilities of teachers and so on should all be so much more relevant (and therefore more interesting) when delivered in the context in which they occur. In addition, graduates may by definition have virtually no knowledge about the need for educational psychologists and social workers and may well need to be brought down to earth about some of the realities of teaching, especially in deprived areas.

In the classroom, subject teachers can very quickly become set in their ways and reluctant to change. A fly on the wall in their lessons who asks critical questions at the end of them must serve to sharpen their performance. At the same time, the fly may have some good ideas which would enhance the mentor's teaching. And as a critical friend to the trainee, especially as he or she makes the inevitable initial mistakes, the same fly should serve to challenge some of their own methods and assumptions.

What are the hallmarks of the good teacher which will also make him or her a good educator? A thorough knowledge of one's subject is a *sine qua non*, but this needs to be allied to an almost proselytising type of enthusiasm to communicate it to others. A thorough knowledge of the syllabus to be covered is distinctly helpful, but the good educator will not be afraid to deviate from it in order to explore side issues as they come up. For example, the study of literature in *any* language will pose questions of life, death, morality, beliefs, relationships and so on. Discussed as they occur and in context can be so much more fruitful (and meaningful) than leaving them, almost as taboos, to be covered as discrete topics in Religious Studies or General Studies. This requires confidence in oneself, and this is one of the most positive benefits which can accrue from teaching practice. The ability to be flexible and to respond to the mood of a class cannot really be *taught*. But carefully controlled and supervised teaching practice, together with the willingness to experiment with techniques and ideas, can create conditions in which the trainee teacher can gain confidence. The ability to improvise and to adapt has much in common with the skills required by an actor and is certainly one of the most important attributes of a successful teacher.

Very little less important than a thorough knowledge of the subject is a knowledge of one's pupils. A good teacher may be able to impart an infinite amount of knowledge in more or less digestible form, but success may be less than complete if the pupils are no more than names in the mark book. No one can teach a potential teacher to like children, but it is important to make him or her aware of the incalculable return to be harvested from getting to know the pupils as individuals, to take a genuine interest in them and to try to understand them. This does not imply trying to be one of them – one of the quickest routes to failure. The opportunity to be involved with the holistic business of education during teaching practice and to see by practical rather than by theoretical means the subtle inter-relationship between theory and practice is one of the most valuable aspects of SCITT.

Sceptics may raise the argument that independent school parents are paying handsomely for their children to be taught by qualified teachers rather than by trainees. There can be little doubt, however, that some trainees may even be better than some qualified teachers. In addition, pupils usually have much to gain by listening to a different voice and by following a different approach. The crucial factor is effective and constant supervision and monitoring and that is one of the areas where the Consortium Consultant and the Consortium Co-ordinator have a particularly important role to play.

Very soon after HMC had put in place its programme of inspection, it was realised that participation in an inspection was one of the best possible means of delivering INSET and of broadening experience. Indeed, this has been one of the principal arguments used to persuade Heads who have been reluctant to release their teachers for inspections. Participation in SCITT will achieve a very similar purpose to inspection.

It is stating the blindingly obvious to say that the future of education depends on the supply of teachers of quality. Independent school Heads cannot afford to sit back and blame the government for the low number of suitable applicants for that Physics or Mathematics or Technology post, if they are not prepared to make their own contribution to the supply and training of teachers. The latter is a problem of education as a whole, not simply of the maintained or the independent sectors. If altruism is not in favour with hard-headed boards of governors, then the sheer pragmatism of having the opportunity to take first pick of a batch of enthusiastic trainees ought to merit consideration. And since the ideal SCITT consortium will be composed of a mixture of HMC, GSA and SHA schools, perhaps even with IAPS and/or primary schools, the opportunity to bridge the gap between the maintained and the independent sectors is enormous.

It can be argued that the really inspiring teachers are 'born' rather than 'made': they have wide-ranging and sharp minds, know not only their own subject but also how it relates to others, present their teaching in an interesting (perhaps even exciting) way and are able to establish a strong rapport with their pupils. These paragons will in most cases be humble enough to acknowledge that their own learning process never ends and that they *can* learn from a course of professional training. The middle of the road teacher is likely to have the right intentions and instincts but needs to have them developed and sharpened. Inevitably, a small number of unsuitable candidates will slip through the most rigorous selection procedures, but how much better for everyone that they should be weeded out very quickly, ideally with some guidance about a more suitable career, rather than that they should be unleashed on a more permanent basis on unsuspecting classes and have to suffer the greater humiliation of being dismissed.

I would not wish to turn the clock back to 1959 nor to have to take again my first faltering steps in the classroom. However, I believe that I would have found immensely valuable the sort of SCITT courses which are now available. Although SCITT would not be the right choice for *all* trainees, it does offer most aspiring teachers a course ideally balanced between the practice of teaching and the acquisition both of knowledge and experience in the theory of education. I wonder how many teachers, indeed how many Heads, would emerge with an acceptable "er-um" rating from the rough and ready litmus test which I cynically applied to my own PGCE course in 1959!

Chapter 11

Monitoring departments: defining Value Added

Vivian Anthony

Secretary, Headmasters' and Headmistresses' Conference

There was a time when Heads and Heads of Department remained happily sunning themselves on beaches in the South of France or gently meandering down the Dordogne in a canoe until the end of August: sadly, no longer. Come the third week in August discussions will be underway on the results of the A and AS level examinations. Worried or exulting students and parents will be wanting advice as their plans change. Heads will want to know if results are up to expectation. Enquiries and appeals go off to Exam Boards; results are sent to ISIS for publication. In some departments results will have exceeded expectations and in others the reverse will be true. Soon the Head will be preparing a report for governors explaining why results were better or worse than in previous years and why the dreaded league table position is what it is and, usually, why it does not mean what it appears to mean.

For years there have been schemes used by Heads and Directors of Studies to analyse exam results at all levels. It may be true that a department with the poorest results always attracts the least able pupils but if these pupils are performing better in other subjects then some further explanation is needed. The Head of Department will be aware that some teachers in the department are doing better than others but, again, there will be differences in the abilities of pupils in different teaching groups. Governors will hear the Head explaining that the neighbouring school, which has done better in the league tables, is much more fortunate not only because its pupils are more able but because they come from more affluent homes where there are more books and better IT facilities. Moreover, their parents take more interest and are able to offer their children more expert help. They suffer less from family break-up and have fewer pupils from backgrounds where they take education less seriously. They have fewer truants or pupils with behaviour problems.

These are just a few of the problems and excesses regularly discussed by those in schools who are searching for improved performance and higher standards, and surely that includes all Heads and Heads of Department. All-round pupil achievement is seen as the be-all and end-all of school improvement and strategies are needed to bring it about. We must have a good idea of how well we are doing now

Vivian Anthony (left), the Secretary of HMC, was Chairman of the Academic Policy Sub-Committee 1988-1990. He was Headmaster of Colfe's School and Chief Examiner in A Level Economics for the Oxford and Cambridge Board. He lectures on professional development and works closely with QCA, OFSTED and the Exam Boards. He also edited Head to Head. *He is pictured here with Roger Griffiths, recently retired HMC Membership Secretary, and Gillian Shephard, the former Secretary of State for Education.*

before we can plan for improvement. This action will be informed by comparisons with past performance and with other similar schools.

This benchmarking is all the rage but finding schools with sufficient similar circumstances is not that easy. Schools like to emphasise their uniqueness. However, awareness of past improvements and what has been achieved elsewhere is not a bad basis for planning what might be achieved in the coming academic year. Why are some departments in the school doing better than others? Why are some groups of pupils doing better than others? How can efforts be made more effective? Setting demanding but realistic targets is the job of truly professional Heads and Heads of Departments. We must have good accurate information on which to base the strategies for achieving these targets as well as the mechanisms for reviewing progress.

This philosophy and practice is fundamental to the case for measuring 'value-added' in our schools.

All schools, but especially those in the independent sector, argue that success in educating pupils has to do with much more than good examination results. Of course some things in education can be measured more easily than others. Some outcomes can be analysed objectively, others are open to subjective judgements. Dominic Milroy, former Chairman of HMC and former Headmaster of Ampleforth, remarked that the most important aspects of education cannot be measured. Parents, in saner moments, would agree that the most important test is what sort of person their son or daughter turns out to be. Have they had the right values inculcated? Did they enjoy their time at schools and go on to be happy and fulfilled adults? Were they prepared for lifelong learning? More immediately parents want to know why examination grades were not high enough to enable their child to win a place at a prestigious university.

In seeking to provide a broad and balanced education, schools have developed a wide range of activities and structures. All of these make demands on the scarce resources which have to be allocated by Heads or their senior and middle managers. Decisions to direct or encourage staff to spend time and resources on one activity rather than another are implicitly or explicitly based on the belief that the one adds more value to the education provided than the other. There must be many Heads and Heads of Departments who wish they had the information to make their decisions more wisely. How many times have I heard colleagues say that the geography results would be better if members of that department spent less time worrying about the performance of their school rugby team and more about the quality of the academic work of their pupils?

Inspection has helped to sharpen our thinking in this respect and a good deal of re-thinking has followed the recommendations in inspection reports. Inspectors want to know that pupils' achievements are at least commensurate with their ability. OFSTED produce PANDA (Performance and Assessment) reports for maintained schools using data distilled from inspection findings. A massive database enables OFSTED to tell schools how they compare with others. School management teams are encouraged to use this benchmark information to set targets for school improvement. OFSTED's publication *School Evaluation Matters* argues that 'schools that regularly evaluate their own performance make greater improvements and maintain higher standards than others.'

While discussions about 'value-added' refer to much more than academic performance it is on this that much of the argument is currently centred, despite the contention elsewhere in the book that this emphasis is giving way to a national obsession and taking from the independent sector a certain uniqueness. Much as we deplore the impact on the breadth and quality of education of the introduction of examination performance league tables, we have to acknowledge the increased attention given to achievement which may have contributed to some improvement in grades, although there is also evidence that some A levels have become easier.

Whilst there may well be a connection between publication and improvement, the extent of this 'improvement' is difficult to ascertain. John Clare, of *The Daily Telegraph*, who claims to have fathered the tables in the teeth of opposition from Heads, will gain some satisfaction from this, though his A level tables, based on A and B grades only, continue to attract hostility from those who believe that performance at all levels should be recognised. There should be as much satisfaction in a student of very modest ability achieving a C grade as there is in an able candidate gaining an A grade. This is what value-added calculations are about: but note the *Telegraph's* health warning 'Labour should beware of its commitment to new value-added tables which ... would merely muddy the results. It will be hard to decide what factors should be taken into account ... Parents are perfectly capable of making allowances for local conditions.' The CEM Centre (see below) calculations do not reflect sociological factors.

HMC can take some credit for tidying up the process of publishing exam results. Most schools had been publishing results for years but were being picked off one by one by the press who then produced tables which were often in the realms of fantasy. The ISIS table of results is at least based on a set of clear rules which ensure that all schools are treated alike. For those who believe that A level General Studies results should be included, separate tables are produced. Moreover, there is none of the nonsense perpetrated by the DfEE of including only the results achieved by pupils in a particular age group, so that a school like Winchester, which would be in most peoples' top five year on year, comes out seventh or lower in Hampshire.

The impression is given that all independent schools have a selected entry. Some self-selection based on ability to pay is ameliorated by the award of scholarships and bursaries but many schools, particularly in the boarding sector, have very few candidates from whom to choose. Some schools have to take those pupils rejected by more prestigious competitors. As a result the difference in overall levels of ability of pupils on entry varies widely from school to school. Professor Carol Fitz-Gibbon commented: "The difference between state schools and the independent sector is largely in terms of wealth and wealth is not strongly correlated with ability (generally found in most Western countries). This does indeed mean that the independent schools have a wide range of ability of pupils on entry."

Yet these differences between schools are ignored by those comparing schools' performance on the basis of raw examination results. Even experienced commentators like John Rae, former Headmaster of Westminster, thunder about the poor performance of independent schools with a low position in the league tables. Poor performance there may be in some cases but in others schools will be doing a good job with weak pupils. A level courses are not well suited to pupils below the top third of the ability range: there are many pupils outside that range in our schools and very often they are skilfully guided through the minefield to obtain results beyond what could be expected from their ability. It is this relationship between ability and expectations which is central to calculations of value-added. Alternative representation of examination results in these cases may do something to restore the balance and to inform critics.

The National Foundation for Educational Research, Moray House, SIMS and similar organisations offer good systems for calculating value-added but more HMC schools have been working with The Curriculum, Evaluation and Management Centre, now at the University of Durham. Professor Fitz-Gibbon, its Director, is a leading player in the game. ALIS, the A Level Information Scheme, began in 1983 and the Centre offers schemes for all age groups. They have YELLIS for Year 11 pupils; MidYlS for Middle Years 7, 8 and 9; and PIPS, Performance Indicators in Primary Schools. Professor Fitz-Gibbon has also advised the DfEE and SCAA on a system related to Key Stage test results and beginning with a baseline test on entry to primary school at five years.

All pupils in HMC schools in England and Wales took a baseline test (MidYIS) on entry to their senior school in 1997 at either 11+ or 13+. The test is made up of seven elements: mathematics, vocabulary, perceptual speed and accuracy, cross-sections, proof-reading, block counting and picture tests. Both aptitude and prior attainment are tested but it is designed principally to provide a good prediction of performance at GCSE. With information coming from hundreds of thousands of candidates in trials and actual tests, the psychometric qualities of the test have been honed. There is a second test for Year 7 pupils which is designed to differentiate further pupils' abilities and to help schools in which ability on entry is skewed towards either end of the ability range. There are different versions of the test – high, middle and low ability – assigned to candidates on the basis of their performance in the first test. The second test also incorporates a short questionnaire which provides schools with information about pupils' support for learning in the home, aspirations for the future, career choice and intentions on continuing education.

Schools want to know how their pupils are performing in relation to pupils of similar ability elsewhere. To help in this process, scores of MidYIS and other tests are standardised to a mean of 100 and a standard deviation of 15. A pupil scoring exactly in line with the national average will score 100. Statisticians will be interested in the reliability and validity of the MidYIS test. Preliminary results indicate reliability as numerical 0.93, verbal (vocabulary) 0.89, non-verbal (pattern recognition and spatial aptitude) 0.90 and skills 0.88. Predictive validity, based on correlations of the test with KS3 results, was shown to be for English 0.68, maths 0.78 and science 0.74. By plotting pupils' scores in this baseline test against those pupils' GCSE results MidYIS is capable of providing users with a great deal of information from comparing the performance of pupils, classes, departments and schools with norms for schools across the nation and also for independent schools. Performance can be plotted against regression lines for GCSE as a whole and for individual subjects. Regression lines (see page 102) provide a clear representation on a graph of the national trend.

In addition to HMC schools, many in GSA, in SHMIS and in maintained schools take part in this scheme for calculating value-added in secondary schools up to GCSE. Schools can compare their performance by plotting scores against either a national regression line for all candidates or against the line for independent schools only. The same will be possible in each individual subject. IAPS want a complementary system for preparatory schools. The CEM Centre provides a genuine and reputable alternative to the system operated by the DfEE/QCA for state schools, which measures value-added as the progress made by pupils from one Key Stage test to another. HMC considered Key Stage test levels to be too blunt to be helpful. If most pupils are achieving the same level comparisons become meaningless. Conversely, there was little confidence in the accuracy of the actual marks giving rise to the levels. The CEM Centre found that marks awarded by teachers varied from school to school so HMC and GSA decided to adopt the idea of a specifically designed test on entry. We have no difficulty in accepting the conclusions of the team which undertook the project on which SCAA's advice to the Secretary in 1997 was based:

> "Value-added analyses can be useful to schools in evaluating their effectiveness by providing them with information about how their pupils have progressed relative to others. They ... give ... a truer picture of a school's performance than can be done through raw results alone."

> "Value-added analyses compare the progress made by individual pupils and groups of pupils between two stages in their education with the average progress made by all pupils. This allows schools to determine the extent to which their pupils have made the progress expected of them over that period."

In this latter function, value-added analysis is an essential tool for a Head and Head of Department. Schools are capable of producing their own analysis of results but the advantage of a national system is that it allows schools to compare themselves with schools in other areas on the basis of the same tests and the same analyses. It was for this reason that many schools decided to join ALIS which compares performance at GCSE with that achieved by the same pupils at A level. The CEM

Centre produced two schemes: the full ALIS and the basic version. If a school believes a student's true ability is not reflected by their GCSE performance, they can administer the International Test of Developed Abilities as an alternative base-line measure.

Schools are provided with bar charts for each GCSE subject showing how average performance compared with the previous year. The distribution of departments' student abilities on intake show which departments had intakes above or below the average. A further ALIS bar chart shows which departments' raw A levels were above or below the average. One simple technique for determining value-added is based on calculating residual scores; these are the differences between actual and expected A level results. For example, if Tom Jones's average GCSE results predict that he will obtain a B grade in A level English (*ie* eight points) but he actually obtains an A grade (ten points), then his residual score would be +2. If Sally Thomas obtains a C grade when her prediction was a B, then her residual score would be -2.

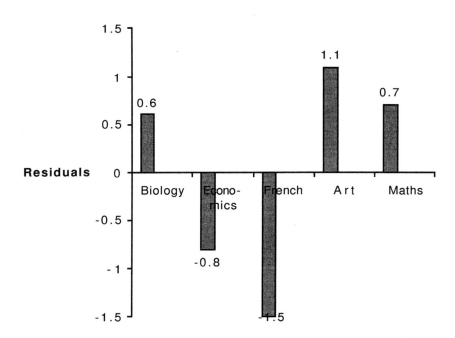

Residuals are calculated for all pupils in all subjects and bar charts can be drawn for the department showing how overall actual scores differed from expected scores. Again, departments can be shown to be performing better or worse than average.

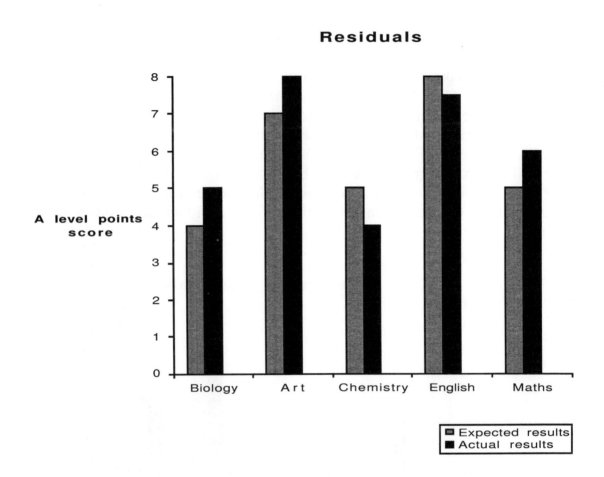

Another piece of helpful information is provided by a 'chances graph' which shows the distribution of A level grades achieved by pupils starting from the same level of average GCSE score. This is particularly welcomed by teachers as an antidote to a single predicted grade. The visualisation of the chance of every grade is more realistic and more acceptable since it does not seem to close down options or expectations. As an illustration, the hypothetical percentage of candidates with an average GCSE score of between 5.5 and 7.0 gaining each grade in A level history in 1997.

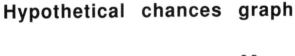

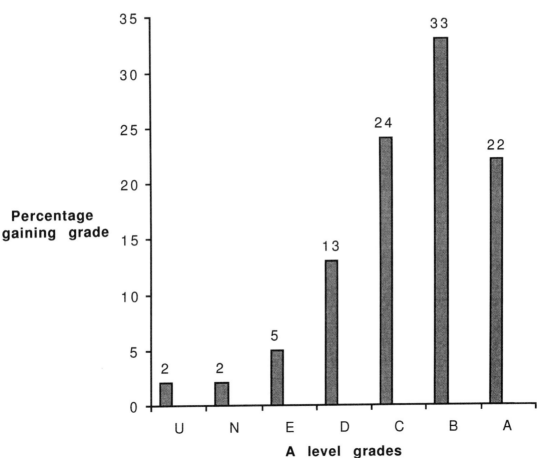

Most Heads of Departments find the use of a regression line gives the clearest analysis. On a graph with the vertical axis showing A level points scores in the given subject and a horizontal axis showing the average GCSE scores of those candidates a regression line is drawn giving the predictions based on the total national sample. Each candidate's score in that department is entered as a dot and the value-added in each case can be measured by looking at the vertical distance between the dots and the line. Those dots above the line have exceeded expectations.

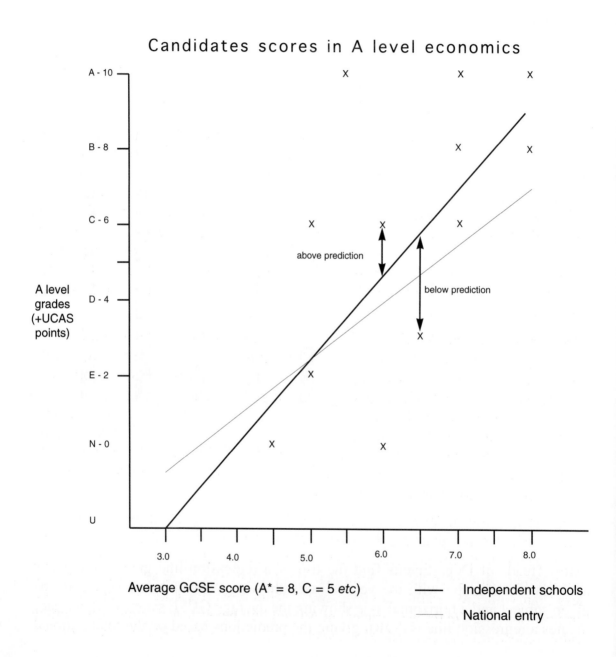

Candidates' average GCSE score	A level points prediction	Points scored	Residual
8	9	10	+1
8	9	8	-1
7	7	10	+3
7	7	8	+1
7	7	6	-1
6.5	6	4	-2
6	4	6	+2
5.5	3	10	+7
5	2	2	0
5	2	6	+4
4.5	0	0	-1

And what should Heads and Heads of Departments do with all this information? Possibly value added data will only confirm what is already known about the strengths and weaknesses of the school. It will though bring greater precision and clarity to the questions "where are we now?" and "how do we plan to improve on this position?" The reason why the French department is doing less well than the maths department may be due to the weakness of an individual teacher or to the way the department as a whole is managed. The teacher may be achieving success with pupils of average ability but is failing those at either end of the ability range. That teacher would benefit from INSET aimed at improved teaching method in differentiation.

If students have completed a CEM Centre Attitude Survey, other relevant information might be available. Students may claim the library is a difficult place to work in because it is noisy and overcrowded. Lessons occur in rooms where specialist equipment is not available. There was insufficient guidance on how to study or advice in choosing the right subject. Perhaps some of the underperforming students spent a great deal of time in drama productions and other activities, including theatre visits. In this department the number of students who claimed to enjoy classes and to get on well with the teachers was lower than in other departments. However, such factors are to be included in calculations.

Some Heads will be able to report to parents and governors that their value-added was much greater than might appear from raw exam results. Clearly in any rearrangement of tables of school performance there will be as many losers as there are winners. However, the differences in performance in value-added terms will be less than with raw results. Some of those schools with average candidate scores around 18 points (ie three C grades) at A level will nevertheless show considerable value added because their students low average scores at GCSE. Other schools with average scores around 30 points (*ie* three A grades) may not have added much more value because their students had very high grades, perhaps straight A or A*, at GCSE. Of course, the ALIS system allows even those with maximum GCSE grades to add value at A level.

The outstanding results of pupils in the most academic schools are not due simply to the high ability of the students, the quality of the teaching and the general ethos of the school play an important part. Such schools and students have rightly been lauded by the media for setting the highest standards. Carol Fitz-Gibbon suggests the time has now come for the efforts of all schools to be recognised, including those which struggle away successfully with children of few talents and inspire and cajole them to produce results which those pupils would probably not have achieved without the support of the school. Value-added analysis will bring welcome recognition for their efforts.

Chapter 12

Stretching the ablest pupils

James Sabben-Clare

Headmaster, Winchester College

It may seem pedantic and schoolmasterly to start with definitions, but we had better be clear what we are talking about and who we are talking about. 'Stretching' suggests elastic under tension, usually as a result of the ends being pulled apart. The kinds of stretching that I shall be illustrating are in part about widening the scope of mental activity: I shall also be applying the term rather more loosely to the idea of increasing the gradient of difficulty in the work that pupils undertake. I remember a former Master of Churchill College saying to us at a Headmasters' Conference in Cambridge: "It doesn't matter what subject your pupils are studying, or what level they start at. It's the steepness of the gradient that matters."

Identifying these 'able' pupils with any precision is even harder. The Advisory Group to the QCA that is looking into special provision for the able classifies the top 2% of the 16-19 student population as 'exceptionally able' and the top 20% as 'most able'. The criteria which might determine the meaning of 'top' in this context are absent: so I am not much the wiser.

It might be more helpful to put the statistics on one side, and instead to make a stab at identifying the characteristics of pupils generally regarded as bright, or able. It is a truism to say that ability comes in many forms. Nevertheless in the context of academic education, the main indicators are likely to be these: a good, even if selective, memory: intellectual curiosity, with an appetite both for details and for the broader ideas; speed in assimilating material and grasping logical structures: and a facility for making connections, whether logical or associative, and for seeing unusual patterns of thought.

These characteristics in themselves suggest teaching approaches which are likely to be fruitful with able pupils, above all the need to be flexible in terms of both pace and content. Working strictly to a syllabus, even more following a text-book chapter by chapter, is unlikely to provide the stimulus that your pupils are looking for. Of course the syllabus has got to be covered: but that should happen almost incidentally, as a by-product of the intellectual process that you are engaged in. As for exam preparation, that too should not loom too large. Able pupils will tend to be good at exams anyway, and usually enjoy them. The teacher's aim should be to work beyond the strict requirements of the exam, so that when the test comes, the questions are easily within the pupils' compass. Few modern text-books will provide the sort of material that enables you to do this. Most of them are written for a broad middle band of ability, and will therefore have to be used selectively with more able pupils.

This sort of requirement clearly makes great demands on the teacher. To state the obvious once more, effective teaching of able pupils needs equally able teachers; more precisely, teachers with a love of the subject and a delight in communicating that love, teachers with a wide range of interest that will tend to elicit interested questions, then with the confidence to follow the lines of inquiry that those questions give rise to. This may seem a counsel of perfection. Where are such teachers to be found? Perhaps in more places than you would imagine. For I am not talking necessarily about teachers with the highest paper qualifications.

More important than that is an environment in which teachers are encouraged continually to extend their own education through reading and thinking and writing. The game is half won when the pupil realises that he or she is sharing a voyage of intellectual discovery with the teacher. When that relationship is established, the teacher will not mind admitting ignorance or making mistakes in the classroom; for both are a necessary part of the process of learning. Another spin-off of the relationship is that the pupil can then be encouraged to take on the role of teacher from time to time. Getting them to prepare lectures, run the Science or History or Classics Society, write up their ideas, join in conducting seminars or taking classes: all these will help to enlarge their perceptions and clarify their thinking. In terms of transferable skills that will be of value to them in later life, few will be more important than the ability to put thoughts together and express them effectively.

Apart from their teachers, the other people from whom able pupils will derive stimulus are their peers. It is much harder for ability to be nurtured in isolation than in a group of equals. Again perhaps we are looking to an ideal, since (obviously) the higher the degree of giftedness, the more rarely it is found. Few schools can expect to have large concentrations of intellectual talent. But at least you will be doing your best for your ablest pupils if you set them according to ability. This seems to be less important in the Humanities than in other branches of learning: but in subjects where most of the teaching aims to build up knowledge and understanding by repetition, and by exposition in simple steps, the abler pupils may become impatient of such deliberate methods. They need the steeper gradient.

The way you group pupils is one structural factor in the strategy for teaching the ablest: the way the curriculum is devised is another. Giving your teachers the freedom and encouragement to range over their subject and not be inhibited by exam requirements is, I have suggested, as important as anything. Taking this principle further, you may achieve even more if you can insist that the curriculum has built into it areas of work which are not exam-related, and which you can show that you still take just as seriously as those that are. What most schools call Sixth Form General Studies is a case in point. Teaching it in penny packages, with a taster here and a module there, is not likely to be much of a stimulus. If you can create out of it a more substantial course of study, with serious reading and writing an integral part, you may spark off an interest for life, and provide an element of education which is remembered and savoured long after the A level syllabuses have been forgotten.

You will be able to find more room for this sort of teaching if you are in a position to persuade your colleagues to reduce the GCSE courses (in length or number or both), and brave enough to limit the number of periods for teaching

James Sabben-Clare is the Chairman-elect of HMC. He was a scholar of Winchester College and later returned to become Head of the Classics department, Master in Charge of Scholars' House, and since 1985 Headmaster. For HMC he has been principally involved in Academic Policy and Inspections.

an A level subject to, say, seven a week. If some of the GCSEs are got out of the way early, so that the whole of the Fifth Form year is not then swamped with exam work, you may be able to provide some interesting free-standing options in the gap thus created. At the same time you are sending out the message that education is about more than accumulating certificates.

These general observations are derived not just from my own experience of being in a school with quite a high proportion of able pupils, but also from the accumulated wisdom of my colleagues at Winchester. The Heads of various Departments have been kind enough to put together some ideas about how their subjects may best be taught to the most able. I offer them with grateful acknowledgement, and in the hope that a few at least may be profitably adopted elsewhere.

Mathematics is the subject in which special ability often shows earliest. You therefore need strategies in place for dealing with it from the lowest forms. Setting by ability is important, the size of the top set being determined by the number that can move together comfortably at the same pace. New topics should be introduced with an interesting problem that will start discussion going and elicit the central ideas from the pupils themselves by means of a Socratic dialogue. The topic does not have to be neatly finished off all in one sequence: incompleteness can leave room for the students to ponder and question further. Drawing matters together in a logical order can be done much later. The teacher knows in advance where he wants to get to, but should not mind changing direction several times along the way in response to questions or a feeling for tangential points that would be interesting to explore.

The teaching of **Science** is more beset by syllabus constraints than most subjects. The Key Stage 4 Sc1 investigation is a particular blight on imaginative teaching. The only ways to avoid them are by taking radical measures: restrict the number of public exams and get them out of the way early, look at alternative syllabuses (like IGCSE instead of GCSE), and create space for teachers to do their own thing. Develop a wide range of activities and teaching styles, including plenty of practical work. Bring in outside experts for Colloquia and Symposia. Involve your nearest university department through visits and lectures: if you are lucky, you may be able to get surplus equipment from them, like an NMR spectrometer. Your facilities need to be as good as you can make them and available whenever pupils might want them.

What characterises special ability in **English** is wide reading and the development of a precise and individual critical voice. Spending leisure time with a good book rather than a computer game may be against the contemporary culture; but some children will have an appetite for it and they need to be encouraged. Discuss their interests with them, get them into libraries; consider giving up Eng Lit GCSE (at least you would be saved all the demands for re-marks) and devising your own literature syllabus instead. At the Sixth Form level, again encourage independent reading, away from the A level texts, and follow this up with individual tutorials. Set up a Literature Prize Essay for the same purpose. Get them to teach lessons and lead seminars. Encourage creative writing, perhaps for an in-house publication. Involve them in the writing and producing of plays. Invite leading novelists, poets, playwrights, as well as academics, to come and talk. Take them to good stage productions. Let them see and hear the best literary expression of English there is to be found.

Classics is historically the subject most used for stretching ability. It lends itself readily for the purpose because of the wide range of difficulty to be found in Latin and Greek authors. If your pupils find Caesar too easy, let them try Tacitus; if they can skip through Xenophon, they will have to scratch their heads over the speeches in Thucydides. Get beyond the A level syllabuses: read whole plays in Greek, not just the Easy Excerpts; tackle some of the harder poets: discuss them as literature not just as intellectual puzzles. To develop a wide and sensitive understanding of the languages, do some good old-fashioned (*ie* difficult) Unseens and Proses. Even try some Verse composition: they often love it. Give classes on some of the by-ways of classical culture and language – inscriptions, metre, triremes, or whatever – and extend this through outside speakers. Because you are dealing with whole civilisations, the range is infinite.

Modern Languages invite much of the same treatment as English and Classics combined. Teaching should be based on sound, indeed sophisticated, knowledge of grammatical structures; and wide reading, not necessarily restricted to literary topics. Encouragement may be through Prize Essays and Speech Prizes; putting on foreign language plays: and the compilation of dossiers (sets of exercises, articles, videos *etc*) on particular topics by the teachers. Technology now plays an increasingly important part, through the use of the Language Laboratory, Satellite TV, and the Internet. But nothing is a substitute for spending time in the foreign countries concerned. So exchanges and study visits have to be part of your programme.

In **History** and related disciplines able pupils should be encouraged to pursue their own interests and develop their own ideas about them. This requires rigorous examination of evidence, wide reading, and imagination in the construction of hypotheses. Quite a range of aptitudes come into play, and the same pupil is not likely to be equally strong in all of them. The role of the teacher is to help fill out the process, by guiding the questions (without minding if they seem to be too discursive), suggesting further reading, and testing the argumentation. Ideally this will happen in a one-to-one tutorial context. Shared exploration of a subject by these means on a regular basis is a far more effective preparation for university admission interviews than any of those mock-interview programmes we all put our pupils through.

I have nothing to say about **Computer Studies** because that is an area where the pupils are often more expert than their teachers and will make most of their own running. You are fortunate indeed if you have colleagues who can keep up with them.

The notion that bright pupils will take care of their own education in other respects is demonstrably false. For one thing, not all intelligent children are self-motivating. They are likely to benefit from good teaching as much as anyone else. The trouble is, they often need a different, more individual sort of teaching, and this is expensive in manpower. Special Needs at the opposite end of the academic spectrum have long been recognised, and most schools are prepared to make provision for them. The special needs of the gifted are no less important for the education of the next generation and there should be incentives for all schools to invest in them.